TEACHER'S PET PUBLICATIONS

PUZZLE PACK
for
Witness

based on the book by
Karen Hesse

Written by
Mary B. Collins

INTRODUCTION
If you already own the LitPlan for this title, this Puzzle Pack will refresh your Unit Resource Materials and Vocabulary Resource Materials sections plus give you additional materials you can substitute into the tests.If you do not already have a complete LitPlan, these pages will give you some supplemental materials to use with your own plan. There are two main groups of materials: one set for unit words (such as characters' names, symbols, places, etc.) and one set for vocabulary words associated with the book.

WORD LIST
There is a word list for both the unit words and the vocabulary words. These lists show you which words are being used in the materials and the clues or definitions being used for those words. You may want to give students a word list with clues/definitions to help them, or you may want students to only have a word list (without clues/definitions) if you want them to work a little harder. Both are available for duplication. The word lists can also be your "calling key" for the bingo games.

FILL IN THE BLANK AND MATCHING
There are 4 each of the fill in the blank and matching worksheets for both the unit and vocabulary words. These pages can be used either as extra worksheets for students or as objective parts of a unit test. They can be done individually if students need extra help or as a whole class activity to review the material covered.

MAGIC SQUARES
The magic squares not only reinforce the material covered but also work on reasoning and math skills. Many teachers have told us that their students really enjoy doing these!

WORD SEARCH PUZZLES
The word search words go in all directions, as indicated on your answer keys. Two of the word search puzzles have the clues listed rather than the words. This makes the puzzle a little more difficult, but it reinforces the material better. Two word search puzzles have words only for students who find the clue puzzles too difficult.

CROSSWORD PUZZLES
Both unit and vocabulary word sections have 4 crossword puzzles.

BINGO CARDS
There are 32 individual bingo cards for the unit words and 32 individual bingo cards for the vocabulary words. You can use your word list as a "call list," calling the words at random and marking them off of your list as you go, or you could use the flash cards by cutting them apart and drawing the words at random from a hat (or box or whatever). To make a better review, you might ask for the definition and spelling of each word as you call it out–or you could call out the definitions and have students tell you the words they need to look for on the puzzle.

JUGGLE LETTERS
The vocabulary juggle letter game is intended to help students learn the spellings of the words. One sheet has the definitions listed on it as an extra help for students who need it or to reinforce the definitions if you choose to do so.

FLASH CARDS
We've included a set of vocabulary flash cards you can duplicate, cut, and fold for your students. Some teachers make a few sets for general use by the class; others make a set for each student. Some teachers duplicate them for each student and have the students cut & fold their own. You can cut out just the words and put them in a hat, have each student pick out one word and write the definition and a sentence for that word. Students then swap words and papers, with the next student adding a sentence of his own under the last one. You can have students swap as many times as you like. Each time the student will read the sentences written prior to his own and then add a sentence. You can cut out the words and definitions separately and play "I Have; Who Has?" Each student in the room draws a word and definition. The first student says, "I have (the name of the word). Who has the definition?" The student with the definition reads it then says, "I have (the name of the vocabulary word she has). Who has the definition?" The round continues until all words and definitions have been given.

No.	Word	Clue/Definition
1.	BABY	Percelle found one wrapped in a newspaper.
2.	BRANDED	The KKK did this to Johnny with the letters KKK.
3.	BRIDGE	Johnny Reeves jumps off a __________ because he is afraid of the Klan.
4.	BROOMS	Sale items that caused a stampede
5.	CANE	Mr. Field's weapon at the courhouse
6.	CAR	Klansmen stole this from Merlin.
7.	COLLEGE	Iris paid for her siblings to go there.
8.	CROSS	The KKK burns one on July 4th.
9.	ESTHER	Saw the person who shot Ira Hirsh
10.	FEAR	Merlin runs away because he feels this.
11.	FIELD	Leanora helps him and they become friends.
12.	FITZGERALD	Helps save Ira Hirsh
13.	FRANKS	Rich, white boy who was murdered
14.	GALOSHES	Mary struts around in these.
15.	HARVEY	____ begins to have doubts about the Klan when they get more violent.
16.	HATE	Characteristic of Klan members
17.	HEAVEN	Esther thinks her mother took a train to this place.
18.	HIRSH	Klan thinks this family is worse than the Sutters.
19.	HOLLOWEEN	Holiday Esther enjoys celebrating
20.	HOME	Johnny says women are happiest at this place.
21.	HOTEL	Place where Harvey and Klan do damage
22.	IRA	Owns a shoe store in town
23.	IRIS	Is a bootlegger on the side to earn extra money
24.	JERRY	Sara's dog that is killed by the Klan
25.	JEWS	Group the Klan targets
26.	JOHNNY	Shot Ira Hirsh
27.	KELLER	Leanora gets a signed book from her.
28.	KIDNAPPING	Merlin is charged with this.
29.	KKK	Group that harasses people in the town
30.	LEANORA	Clears Merlin's name
31.	LEOPOLD	_________ and Loeb kill a teenage boy in Chicago.
32.	LEWIS	Was suffocated by a sandbank cave-in
33.	MARRIED	Sara never did this.
34.	MARY	Wants to be married in KKK robes
35.	MERLIN	Tries to rescue his girlfriend from the orphanage
36.	MURDER	Leopold and Loeb are charged with this.
37.	NEWSPAPER	Where the town learns how Leanora rescued Esther
38.	PERCELLE	Person in charge of maintaining peace in the town
39.	PETTIBONE	Hassles Leanora about her race
40.	POISON	Merlin was supposed to put this in the Sutters' well.
41.	POOR	The Klan gives money to them.
42.	PRESIDENT	Coolidge was elected as this.
43.	REEVES	Was kicked out of the KKK
44.	REYNARD	He gives Merlin the keys to his business.
45.	ROCK	Someone threw this through Sara's window.
46.	SARA	She is like a mother to Esther.
47.	SCHOOL	Place where Leanora is most often teased about being black
48.	SUTTER	She was stuck in a wagon in the cold for too long and later died: Mrs. _____.
49.	TRAIN	Esther is almost hit by one of these

No. Word	Clue/Definition
50. VIOLA	Does not approve of her husband's involvement with the Klan
51. VOTE	What women got the right to do; Iris Weaver was excited to do this
52. WAGON	No one would help Leanora's family when they had a problem withthis.

Witness Fill In The Blanks 1

_______________ 1. Does not approve of her husband's involvement with the Klan

_______________ 2. Characteristic of Klan members

_______________ 3. Mary struts around in these.

_______________ 4. Shot Ira Hirsh

_______________ 5. Merlin runs away because he feels this.

_______________ 6. Wants to be married in KKK robes

_______________ 7. Tries to rescue his girlfriend from the orphanage

_______________ 8. Coolidge was elected as this.

_______________ 9. Where the town learns how Leanora rescued Esther

_______________ 10. What women got the right to do; Iris Weaver was excited to do this

_______________ 11. Is a bootlegger on the side to earn extra money

_______________ 12. Esther is almost hit by one of these

_______________ 13. Klansmen stole this from Merlin.

_______________ 14. The KKK burns one on July 4th.

_______________ 15. Was suffocated by a sandbank cave-in

_______________ 16. Sara's dog that is killed by the Klan

_______________ 17. Place where Leanora is most often teased about being black

_______________ 18. Saw the person who shot Ira Hirsh

_______________ 19. She was stuck in a wagon in the cold for too long and later died: Mrs. ______.

_______________ 20. The Klan gives money to them.

Witness Fill In The Blanks 1 Answer Key

Answer	Clue
VIOLA	1. Does not approve of her husband's involvement with the Klan
HATE	2. Characteristic of Klan members
GALOSHES	3. Mary struts around in these.
JOHNNY	4. Shot Ira Hirsh
FEAR	5. Merlin runs away because he feels this.
MARY	6. Wants to be married in KKK robes
MERLIN	7. Tries to rescue his girlfriend from the orphanage
PRESIDENT	8. Coolidge was elected as this.
NEWSPAPER	9. Where the town learns how Leanora rescued Esther
VOTE	10. What women got the right to do; Iris Weaver was excited to do this
IRIS	11. Is a bootlegger on the side to earn extra money
TRAIN	12. Esther is almost hit by one of these
CAR	13. Klansmen stole this from Merlin.
CROSS	14. The KKK burns one on July 4th.
LEWIS	15. Was suffocated by a sandbank cave-in
JERRY	16. Sara's dog that is killed by the Klan
SCHOOL	17. Place where Leanora is most often teased about being black
ESTHER	18. Saw the person who shot Ira Hirsh
SUTTER	19. She was stuck in a wagon in the cold for too long and later died: Mrs. ______.
POOR	20. The Klan gives money to them.

Witness Fill In The Blanks 2

1. Group the Klan targets
2. Mr. Field's weapon at the courhouse
3. Clears Merlin's name
4. The KKK did this to Johnny with the letters KKK.
5. ____ begins to have doubts about the Klan when they get more violent.
6. Saw the person who shot Ira Hirsh
7. __________ and Loeb kill a teenage boy in Chicago.
8. Mary struts around in these.
9. Where the town learns how Leanora rescued Esther
10. Sara's dog that is killed by the Klan
11. Sale items that caused a stampede
12. Does not approve of her husband's involvement with the Klan
13. Esther thinks her mother took a train to this place.
14. Iris paid for her siblings to go there.
15. Klansmen stole this from Merlin.
16. Leanora helps him and they become friends.
17. Hassles Leanora about her race
18. Leopold and Loeb are charged with this.
19. He gives Merlin the keys to his business.
20. Wants to be married in KKK robes

Witness Fill In The Blanks 2 Answer Key

Answer	Clue
JEWS	1. Group the Klan targets
CANE	2. Mr. Field's weapon at the courhouse
LEANORA	3. Clears Merlin's name
BRANDED	4. The KKK did this to Johnny with the letters KKK.
HARVEY	5. ____ begins to have doubts about the Klan when they get more violent.
ESTHER	6. Saw the person who shot Ira Hirsh
LEOPOLD	7. __________ and Loeb kill a teenage boy in Chicago.
GALOSHES	8. Mary struts around in these.
NEWSPAPER	9. Where the town learns how Leanora rescued Esther
JERRY	10. Sara's dog that is killed by the Klan
BROOMS	11. Sale items that caused a stampede
VIOLA	12. Does not approve of her husband's involvement with the Klan
HEAVEN	13. Esther thinks her mother took a train to this place.
COLLEGE	14. Iris paid for her siblings to go there.
CAR	15. Klansmen stole this from Merlin.
FIELD	16. Leanora helps him and they become friends.
PETTIBONE	17. Hassles Leanora about her race
MURDER	18. Leopold and Loeb are charged with this.
REYNARD	19. He gives Merlin the keys to his business.
MARY	20. Wants to be married in KKK robes

Witness Fill In The Blanks 3

_______________ 1. Characteristic of Klan members

_______________ 2. Percelle found one wrapped in a newspaper.

_______________ 3. ____ begins to have doubts about the Klan when they get more violent.

_______________ 4. Person in charge of maintaining peace in the town

_______________ 5. Clears Merlin's name

_______________ 6. Merlin is charged with this.

_______________ 7. Coolidge was elected as this.

_______________ 8. Is a bootlegger on the side to earn extra money

_______________ 9. She was stuck in a wagon in the cold for too long and later died: Mrs. _____.

_______________ 10. Sale items that caused a stampede

_______________ 11. Sara never did this.

_______________ 12. Group the Klan targets

_______________ 13. She is like a mother to Esther.

_______________ 14. The KKK burns one on July 4th.

_______________ 15. Merlin was supposed to put this in the Sutters' well.

_______________ 16. Saw the person who shot Ira Hirsh

_______________ 17. Shot Ira Hirsh

_______________ 18. Mary struts around in these.

_______________ 19. Esther thinks her mother took a train to this place.

_______________ 20. Was kicked out of the KKK

Witness Fill In The Blanks 3 Answer Key

Answer	Clue
HATE	1. Characteristic of Klan members
BABY	2. Percelle found one wrapped in a newspaper.
HARVEY	3. ____ begins to have doubts about the Klan when they get more violent.
PERCELLE	4. Person in charge of maintaining peace in the town
LEANORA	5. Clears Merlin's name
KIDNAPPING	6. Merlin is charged with this.
PRESIDENT	7. Coolidge was elected as this.
IRIS	8. Is a bootlegger on the side to earn extra money
SUTTER	9. She was stuck in a wagon in the cold for too long and later died: Mrs. _____.
BROOMS	10. Sale items that caused a stampede
MARRIED	11. Sara never did this.
JEWS	12. Group the Klan targets
SARA	13. She is like a mother to Esther.
CROSS	14. The KKK burns one on July 4th.
POISON	15. Merlin was supposed to put this in the Sutters' well.
ESTHER	16. Saw the person who shot Ira Hirsh
JOHNNY	17. Shot Ira Hirsh
GALOSHES	18. Mary struts around in these.
HEAVEN	19. Esther thinks her mother took a train to this place.
REEVES	20. Was kicked out of the KKK

Witness Fill In The Blanks 4

_______________ 1. Group that harasses people in the town

_______________ 2. __________ and Loeb kill a teenage boy in Chicago.

_______________ 3. Klan thinks this family is worse than the Sutters.

_______________ 4. Rich, white boy who was murdered

_______________ 5. Johnny Reeves jumps off a ___________ because he is afraid of the Klan.

_______________ 6. Place where Leanora is most often teased about being black

_______________ 7. Was kicked out of the KKK

_______________ 8. Person in charge of maintaining peace in the town

_______________ 9. She is like a mother to Esther.

_______________ 10. Hassles Leanora about her race

_______________ 11. Esther thinks her mother took a train to this place.

_______________ 12. Saw the person who shot Ira Hirsh

_______________ 13. Esther is almost hit by one of these

_______________ 14. ____ begins to have doubts about the Klan when they get more violent.

_______________ 15. Helps save Ira Hirsh

_______________ 16. Leanora helps him and they become friends.

_______________ 17. Sara never did this.

_______________ 18. Characteristic of Klan members

_______________ 19. Does not approve of her husband's involvement with the Klan

_______________ 20. Leopold and Loeb are charged with this.

Witness Fill In The Blanks 4 Answer Key

Answer	Clue
KKK	1. Group that harasses people in the town
LEOPOLD	2. __________ and Loeb kill a teenage boy in Chicago.
HIRSH	3. Klan thinks this family is worse than the Sutters.
FRANKS	4. Rich, white boy who was murdered
BRIDGE	5. Johnny Reeves jumps off a ___________ because he is afraid of the Klan.
SCHOOL	6. Place where Leanora is most often teased about being black
REEVES	7. Was kicked out of the KKK
PERCELLE	8. Person in charge of maintaining peace in the town
SARA	9. She is like a mother to Esther.
PETTIBONE	10. Hassles Leanora about her race
HEAVEN	11. Esther thinks her mother took a train to this place.
ESTHER	12. Saw the person who shot Ira Hirsh
TRAIN	13. Esther is almost hit by one of these
HARVEY	14. ____ begins to have doubts about the Klan when they get more violent.
FITZGERALD	15. Helps save Ira Hirsh
FIELD	16. Leanora helps him and they become friends.
MARRIED	17. Sara never did this.
HATE	18. Characteristic of Klan members
VIOLA	19. Does not approve of her husband's involvement with the Klan
MURDER	20. Leopold and Loeb are charged with this.

Witness Matching 1

___ 1. BRIDGE	A. Hassles Leanora about her race
___ 2. MARRIED	B. Where the town learns how Leanora rescued Esther
___ 3. PETTIBONE	C. Mr. Field's weapon at the courhouse
___ 4. TRAIN	D. Merlin was supposed to put this in the Sutters' well.
___ 5. BABY	E. Klan thinks this family is worse than the Sutters.
___ 6. GALOSHES	F. Is a bootlegger on the side to earn extra money
___ 7. SARA	G. He gives Merlin the keys to his business.
___ 8. NEWSPAPER	H. Mary struts around in these.
___ 9. BRANDED	I. Group that harasses people in the town
___10. ROCK	J. Esther is almost hit by one of these
___11. JOHNNY	K. What women got the right to do; Iris Weaver was excited to do this
___12. BROOMS	L. Someone threw this through Sara's window.
___13. REYNARD	M. She is like a mother to Esther.
___14. MARY	N. Shot Ira Hirsh
___15. IRIS	O. Does not approve of her husband's involvement with the Klan
___16. VIOLA	P. Owns a shoe store in town
___17. IRA	Q. Was kicked out of the KKK
___18. CROSS	R. Sale items that caused a stampede
___19. REEVES	S. Percelle found one wrapped in a newspaper.
___20. KKK	T. The KKK burns one on July 4th.
___21. VOTE	U. The KKK did this to Johnny with the letters KKK.
___22. POISON	V. Johnny Reeves jumps off a ___________ because he is afraid of the Klan.
___23. HIRSH	W. Rich, white boy who was murdered
___24. FRANKS	X. Sara never did this.
___25. CANE	Y. Wants to be married in KKK robes

Witness Matching 1 Answer Key

V - 1. BRIDGE	A. Hassles Leanora about her race
X - 2. MARRIED	B. Where the town learns how Leanora rescued Esther
A - 3. PETTIBONE	C. Mr. Field's weapon at the courhouse
J - 4. TRAIN	D. Merlin was supposed to put this in the Sutters' well.
S - 5. BABY	E. Klan thinks this family is worse than the Sutters.
H - 6. GALOSHES	F. Is a bootlegger on the side to earn extra money
M - 7. SARA	G. He gives Merlin the keys to his business.
B - 8. NEWSPAPER	H. Mary struts around in these.
U - 9. BRANDED	I. Group that harasses people in the town
L - 10. ROCK	J. Esther is almost hit by one of these
N -11. JOHNNY	K. What women got the right to do; Iris Weaver was excited to do this
R -12. BROOMS	L. Someone threw this through Sara's window.
G -13. REYNARD	M. She is like a mother to Esther.
Y -14. MARY	N. Shot Ira Hirsh
F -15. IRIS	O. Does not approve of her husband's involvement with the Klan
O -16. VIOLA	P. Owns a shoe store in town
P -17. IRA	Q. Was kicked out of the KKK
T -18. CROSS	R. Sale items that caused a stampede
Q -19. REEVES	S. Percelle found one wrapped in a newspaper.
I - 20. KKK	T. The KKK burns one on July 4th.
K -21. VOTE	U. The KKK did this to Johnny with the letters KKK.
D -22. POISON	V. Johnny Reeves jumps off a ___________ because he is afraid of the Klan.
E -23. HIRSH	W. Rich, white boy who was murdered
W -24. FRANKS	X. Sara never did this.
C -25. CANE	Y. Wants to be married in KKK robes

Witness Matching 2

___ 1. IRIS	A. Rich, white boy who was murdered
___ 2. IRA	B. Merlin runs away because he feels this.
___ 3. CANE	C. Saw the person who shot Ira Hirsh
___ 4. HOLLOWEEN	D. The Klan gives money to them.
___ 5. HARVEY	E. Johnny Reeves jumps off a ___________ because he is afraid of the Klan.
___ 6. FRANKS	F. Mr. Field's weapon at the courhouse
___ 7. PETTIBONE	G. Hassles Leanora about her race
___ 8. HOME	H. Johnny says women are happiest at this place.
___ 9. MARY	I. Klansmen stole this from Merlin.
___10. KKK	J. Place where Leanora is most often teased about being black
___11. ESTHER	K. Is a bootlegger on the side to earn extra money
___12. CROSS	L. Klan thinks this family is worse than the Sutters.
___13. POOR	M. Place where Harvey and Klan do damage
___14. BRIDGE	N. Wants to be married in KKK robes
___15. FEAR	O. Someone threw this through Sara's window.
___16. VIOLA	P. Owns a shoe store in town
___17. CAR	Q. ____ begins to have doubts about the Klan when they get more violent.
___18. ROCK	R. Sara never did this.
___19. HEAVEN	S. Does not approve of her husband's involvement with the Klan
___20. SCHOOL	T. Esther thinks her mother took a train to this place.
___21. LEOPOLD	U. Percelle found one wrapped in a newspaper.
___22. BABY	V. Holiday Esther enjoys celebrating
___23. HOTEL	W. Group that harasses people in the town
___24. HIRSH	X. __________ and Loeb kill a teenage boy in Chicago.
___25. MARRIED	Y. The KKK burns one on July 4th.

Witness Matching 2 Answer Key

K - 1. IRIS	A. Rich, white boy who was murdered
P - 2. IRA	B. Merlin runs away because he feels this.
F - 3. CANE	C. Saw the person who shot Ira Hirsh
V - 4. HOLLOWEEN	D. The Klan gives money to them.
Q - 5. HARVEY	E. Johnny Reeves jumps off a __________ because he is afraid of the Klan.
A - 6. FRANKS	F. Mr. Field's weapon at the courhouse
G - 7. PETTIBONE	G. Hassles Leanora about her race
H - 8. HOME	H. Johnny says women are happiest at this place.
N - 9. MARY	I. Klansmen stole this from Merlin.
W -10. KKK	J. Place where Leanora is most often teased about being black
C -11. ESTHER	K. Is a bootlegger on the side to earn extra money
Y -12. CROSS	L. Klan thinks this family is worse than the Sutters.
D -13. POOR	M. Place where Harvey and Klan do damage
E -14. BRIDGE	N. Wants to be married in KKK robes
B -15. FEAR	O. Someone threw this through Sara's window.
S -16. VIOLA	P. Owns a shoe store in town
I - 17. CAR	Q. ____ begins to have doubts about the Klan when they get more violent.
O -18. ROCK	R. Sara never did this.
T -19. HEAVEN	S. Does not approve of her husband's involvement with the Klan
J - 20. SCHOOL	T. Esther thinks her mother took a train to this place.
X -21. LEOPOLD	U. Percelle found one wrapped in a newspaper.
U -22. BABY	V. Holiday Esther enjoys celebrating
M -23. HOTEL	W. Group that harasses people in the town
L - 24. HIRSH	X. __________ and Loeb kill a teenage boy in Chicago.
R -25. MARRIED	Y. The KKK burns one on July 4th.

Witness Matching 3

___ 1. HOTEL	A. Was suffocated by a sandbank cave-in
___ 2. LEANORA	B. No one would help Leanora's family when they had a problem withthis.
___ 3. SARA	C. Clears Merlin's name
___ 4. VIOLA	D. The KKK burns one on July 4th.
___ 5. LEOPOLD	E. Does not approve of her husband's involvement with the Klan
___ 6. LEWIS	F. The KKK did this to Johnny with the letters KKK.
___ 7. MURDER	G. Holiday Esther enjoys celebrating
___ 8. JOHNNY	H. Person in charge of maintaining peace in the town
___ 9. MARRIED	I. Leopold and Loeb are charged with this.
___10. PETTIBONE	J. Merlin is charged with this.
___11. PERCELLE	K. Someone threw this through Sara's window.
___12. BRANDED	L. Klan thinks this family is worse than the Sutters.
___13. WAGON	M. Group that harasses people in the town
___14. HIRSH	N. Sara never did this.
___15. CROSS	O. ____ begins to have doubts about the Klan when they get more violent.
___16. BROOMS	P. Hassles Leanora about her race
___17. HARVEY	Q. Sale items that caused a stampede
___18. FIELD	R. Wants to be married in KKK robes
___19. FRANKS	S. Group the Klan targets
___20. KIDNAPPING	T. She is like a mother to Esther.
___21. KKK	U. Rich, white boy who was murdered
___22. HOLLOWEEN	V. __________ and Loeb kill a teenage boy in Chicago.
___23. MARY	W. Shot Ira Hirsh
___24. JEWS	X. Place where Harvey and Klan do damage
___25. ROCK	Y. Leanora helps him and they become friends.

Witness Matching 3 Answer Key

X - 1. HOTEL	A. Was suffocated by a sandbank cave-in
C - 2. LEANORA	B. No one would help Leanora's family when they had a problem withthis.
T - 3. SARA	C. Clears Merlin's name
E - 4. VIOLA	D. The KKK burns one on July 4th.
V - 5. LEOPOLD	E. Does not approve of her husband's involvement with the Klan
A - 6. LEWIS	F. The KKK did this to Johnny with the letters KKK.
I - 7. MURDER	G. Holiday Esther enjoys celebrating
W - 8. JOHNNY	H. Person in charge of maintaining peace in the town
N - 9. MARRIED	I. Leopold and Loeb are charged with this.
P -10. PETTIBONE	J. Merlin is charged with this.
H -11. PERCELLE	K. Someone threw this through Sara's window.
F -12. BRANDED	L. Klan thinks this family is worse than the Sutters.
B -13. WAGON	M. Group that harasses people in the town
L -14. HIRSH	N. Sara never did this.
D -15. CROSS	O. ____ begins to have doubts about the Klan when they get more violent.
Q -16. BROOMS	P. Hassles Leanora about her race
O -17. HARVEY	Q. Sale items that caused a stampede
Y -18. FIELD	R. Wants to be married in KKK robes
U -19. FRANKS	S. Group the Klan targets
J - 20. KIDNAPPING	T. She is like a mother to Esther.
M -21. KKK	U. Rich, white boy who was murdered
G -22. HOLLOWEEN	V. __________ and Loeb kill a teenage boy in Chicago.
R -23. MARY	W. Shot Ira Hirsh
S -24. JEWS	X. Place where Harvey and Klan do damage
K -25. ROCK	Y. Leanora helps him and they become friends.

Witness Matching 4

___ 1. WAGON	A. She is like a mother to Esther.
___ 2. IRA	B. Leanora helps him and they become friends.
___ 3. VOTE	C. The Klan gives money to them.
___ 4. HOME	D. Johnny says women are happiest at this place.
___ 5. REYNARD	E. No one would help Leanora's family when they had a problem withthis.
___ 6. IRIS	F. Hassles Leanora about her race
___ 7. FITZGERALD	G. He gives Merlin the keys to his business.
___ 8. PETTIBONE	H. Group the Klan targets
___ 9. FIELD	I. The KKK burns one on July 4th.
___10. JOHNNY	J. Clears Merlin's name
___11. CANE	K. __________ and Loeb kill a teenage boy in Chicago.
___12. CROSS	L. What women got the right to do; Iris Weaver was excited to do this
___13. FRANKS	M. Saw the person who shot Ira Hirsh
___14. FEAR	N. Is a bootlegger on the side to earn extra money
___15. SARA	O. Rich, white boy who was murdered
___16. HATE	P. Characteristic of Klan members
___17. ESTHER	Q. Helps save Ira Hirsh
___18. HOLLOWEEN	R. Holiday Esther enjoys celebrating
___19. POOR	S. Merlin runs away because he feels this.
___20. SCHOOL	T. Mr. Field's weapon at the courhouse
___21. LEOPOLD	U. Klansmen stole this from Merlin.
___22. LEANORA	V. Owns a shoe store in town
___23. LEWIS	W. Place where Leanora is most often teased about being black
___24. CAR	X. Shot Ira Hirsh
___25. JEWS	Y. Was suffocated by a sandbank cave-in

Witness Matching 4 Answer Key

E - 1. WAGON	A. She is like a mother to Esther.
V - 2. IRA	B. Leanora helps him and they become friends.
L - 3. VOTE	C. The Klan gives money to them.
D - 4. HOME	D. Johnny says women are happiest at this place.
G - 5. REYNARD	E. No one would help Leanora's family when they had a problem withthis.
N - 6. IRIS	F. Hassles Leanora about her race
Q - 7. FITZGERALD	G. He gives Merlin the keys to his business.
F - 8. PETTIBONE	H. Group the Klan targets
B - 9. FIELD	I. The KKK burns one on July 4th.
X - 10. JOHNNY	J. Clears Merlin's name
T - 11. CANE	K. __________ and Loeb kill a teenage boy in Chicago.
I - 12. CROSS	L. What women got the right to do; Iris Weaver was excited to do this
O - 13. FRANKS	M. Saw the person who shot Ira Hirsh
S - 14. FEAR	N. Is a bootlegger on the side to earn extra money
A - 15. SARA	O. Rich, white boy who was murdered
P - 16. HATE	P. Characteristic of Klan members
M - 17. ESTHER	Q. Helps save Ira Hirsh
R - 18. HOLLOWEEN	R. Holiday Esther enjoys celebrating
C - 19. POOR	S. Merlin runs away because he feels this.
W - 20. SCHOOL	T. Mr. Field's weapon at the courhouse
K - 21. LEOPOLD	U. Klansmen stole this from Merlin.
J - 22. LEANORA	V. Owns a shoe store in town
Y - 23. LEWIS	W. Place where Leanora is most often teased about being black
U - 24. CAR	X. Shot Ira Hirsh
H - 25. JEWS	Y. Was suffocated by a sandbank cave-in

Witness Magic Squares 1

A. KIDNAPPING	E. JOHNNY	I. SARA	M. JERRY
B. ESTHER	F. PETTIBONE	J. VOTE	N. FITZGERALD
C. WAGON	G. SUTTER	K. VIOLA	O. MERLIN
D. GALOSHES	H. CAR	L. LEANORA	P. HOME

1. Hassles Leanora about her race
2. She is like a mother to Esther.
3. Tries to rescue his girlfriend from the orphanage
4. Mary struts around in these.
5. Sara's dog that is killed by the Klan
6. Saw the person who shot Ira Hirsh
7. Klansmen stole this from Merlin.
8. Does not approve of her husband's involvement with the Klan
9. No one would help Leanora's family when they had a problem withthis.
10. Johnny says women are happiest at this place.
11. What women got the right to do; Iris Weaver was excited to do this
12. Shot Ira Hirsh
13. Clears Merlin's name
14. She was stuck in a wagon in the cold for too long and later died: Mrs. _____.
15. Merlin is charged with this.
16. Helps save Ira Hirsh

A=	B=	C=	D=
E=	F=	G=	H=
I=	J=	K=	L=
M=	N=	O=	P=

Witness Magic Squares 1 Answer Key

A. KIDNAPPING	E. JOHNNY	I. SARA	M. JERRY
B. ESTHER	F. PETTIBONE	J. VOTE	N. FITZGERALD
C. WAGON	G. SUTTER	K. VIOLA	O. MERLIN
D. GALOSHES	H. CAR	L. LEANORA	P. HOME

1. Hassles Leanora about her race
2. She is like a mother to Esther.
3. Tries to rescue his girlfriend from the orphanage
4. Mary struts around in these.
5. Sara's dog that is killed by the Klan
6. Saw the person who shot Ira Hirsh
7. Klansmen stole this from Merlin.
8. Does not approve of her husband's involvement with the Klan
9. No one would help Leanora's family when they had a problem withthis.
10. Johnny says women are happiest at this place.
11. What women got the right to do; Iris Weaver was excited to do this
12. Shot Ira Hirsh
13. Clears Merlin's name
14. She was stuck in a wagon in the cold for too long and later died: Mrs. _____.
15. Merlin is charged with this.
16. Helps save Ira Hirsh

A=15	B=6	C=9	D=4
E=12	F=1	G=14	H=7
I=2	J=11	K=8	L=13
M=5	N=16	O=3	P=10

Witness Magic Squares 2

A. VIOLA	E. BROOMS	I. HEAVEN	M. HIRSH
B. KELLER	F. SARA	J. LEANORA	N. PRESIDENT
C. LEWIS	G. HOTEL	K. MARY	O. JERRY
D. IRIS	H. FITZGERALD	L. PETTIBONE	P. HARVEY

1. Leanora gets a signed book from her.
2. Place where Harvey and Klan do damage
3. Wants to be married in KKK robes
4. Coolidge was elected as this.
5. Klan thinks this family is worse than the Sutters.
6. Hassles Leanora about her race
7. Helps save Ira Hirsh
8. Does not approve of her husband's involvement with the Klan
9. ____ begins to have doubts about the Klan when they get more violent.
10. Esther thinks her mother took a train to this place.
11. Sale items that caused a stampede
12. Is a bootlegger on the side to earn extra money
13. Was suffocated by a sandbank cave-in
14. She is like a mother to Esther.
15. Clears Merlin's name
16. Sara's dog that is killed by the Klan

A=	B=	C=	D=
E=	F=	G=	H=
I=	J=	K=	L=
M=	N=	O=	P=

Witness Magic Squares 2 Answer Key

A. VIOLA	E. BROOMS	I. HEAVEN	M. HIRSH
B. KELLER	F. SARA	J. LEANORA	N. PRESIDENT
C. LEWIS	G. HOTEL	K. MARY	O. JERRY
D. IRIS	H. FITZGERALD	L. PETTIBONE	P. HARVEY

1. Leanora gets a signed book from her.
2. Place where Harvey and Klan do damage
3. Wants to be married in KKK robes
4. Coolidge was elected as this.
5. Klan thinks this family is worse than the Sutters.
6. Hassles Leanora about her race
7. Helps save Ira Hirsh
8. Does not approve of her husband's involvement with the Klan
9. ____ begins to have doubts about the Klan when they get more violent.
10. Esther thinks her mother took a train to this place.
11. Sale items that caused a stampede
12. Is a bootlegger on the side to earn extra money
13. Was suffocated by a sandbank cave-in
14. She is like a mother to Esther.
15. Clears Merlin's name
16. Sara's dog that is killed by the Klan

A=8	B=1	C=13	D=12
E=11	F=14	G=2	H=7
I=10	J=15	K=3	L=6
M=5	N=4	O=16	P=9

Witness Magic Squares 3

A. VOTE	E. VIOLA	I. CAR	M. PETTIBONE
B. BRIDGE	F. NEWSPAPER	J. HATE	N. SUTTER
C. BABY	G. HARVEY	K. IRA	O. IRIS
D. REYNARD	H. MARRIED	L. KKK	P. MURDER

1. Hassles Leanora about her race
2. Where the town learns how Leanora rescued Esther
3. Sara never did this.
4. Is a bootlegger on the side to earn extra money
5. Group that harasses people in the town
6. Percelle found one wrapped in a newspaper.
7. What women got the right to do; Iris Weaver was excited to do this
8. Characteristic of Klan members
9. Owns a shoe store in town
10. He gives Merlin the keys to his business.
11. Johnny Reeves jumps off a ___________ because he is afraid of the Klan.
12. Klansmen stole this from Merlin.
13. She was stuck in a wagon in the cold for too long and later died: Mrs. _____.
14. Does not approve of her husband's involvement with the Klan
15. ____ begins to have doubts about the Klan when they get more violent.
16. Leopold and Loeb are charged with this.

A=	B=	C=	D=
E=	F=	G=	H=
I=	J=	K=	L=
M=	N=	O=	P=

Witness Magic Squares 3 Answer Key

A. VOTE	E. VIOLA	I. CAR	M. PETTIBONE
B. BRIDGE	F. NEWSPAPER	J. HATE	N. SUTTER
C. BABY	G. HARVEY	K. IRA	O. IRIS
D. REYNARD	H. MARRIED	L. KKK	P. MURDER

1. Hassles Leanora about her race
2. Where the town learns how Leanora rescued Esther
3. Sara never did this.
4. Is a bootlegger on the side to earn extra money
5. Group that harasses people in the town
6. Percelle found one wrapped in a newspaper.
7. What women got the right to do; Iris Weaver was excited to do this
8. Characteristic of Klan members
9. Owns a shoe store in town
10. He gives Merlin the keys to his business.
11. Johnny Reeves jumps off a ___________ because he is afraid of the Klan.
12. Klansmen stole this from Merlin.
13. She was stuck in a wagon in the cold for too long and later died: Mrs. _____.
14. Does not approve of her husband's involvement with the Klan
15. _____ begins to have doubts about the Klan when they get more violent.
16. Leopold and Loeb are charged with this.

A=7	B=11	C=6	D=10
E=14	F=2	G=15	H=3
I=12	J=8	K=9	L=5
M=1	N=13	O=4	P=16

Witness Magic Squares 4

A. WAGON	E. BRANDED	I. IRA	M. FRANKS
B. LEOPOLD	F. JERRY	J. ROCK	N. HATE
C. CANE	G. VIOLA	K. ESTHER	O. HEAVEN
D. KELLER	H. PETTIBONE	L. HARVEY	P. SARA

1. Hassles Leanora about her race
2. Rich, white boy who was murdered
3. __________ and Loeb kill a teenage boy in Chicago.
4. Saw the person who shot Ira Hirsh
5. Someone threw this through Sara's window.
6. Mr. Field's weapon at the courhouse
7. She is like a mother to Esther.
8. The KKK did this to Johnny with the letters KKK.
9. Esther thinks her mother took a train to this place.
10. Sara's dog that is killed by the Klan
11. Owns a shoe store in town
12. Leanora gets a signed book from her.
13. No one would help Leanora's family when they had a problem withthis.
14. ____ begins to have doubts about the Klan when they get more violent.
15. Does not approve of her husband's involvement with the Klan
16. Characteristic of Klan members

A=	B=	C=	D=
E=	F=	G=	H=
I=	J=	K=	L=
M=	N=	O=	P=

Witness Magic Squares 4 Answer Key

A. WAGON	E. BRANDED	I. IRA	M. FRANKS
B. LEOPOLD	F. JERRY	J. ROCK	N. HATE
C. CANE	G. VIOLA	K. ESTHER	O. HEAVEN
D. KELLER	H. PETTIBONE	L. HARVEY	P. SARA

1. Hassles Leanora about her race
2. Rich, white boy who was murdered
3. __________ and Loeb kill a teenage boy in Chicago.
4. Saw the person who shot Ira Hirsh
5. Someone threw this through Sara's window.
6. Mr. Field's weapon at the courhouse
7. She is like a mother to Esther.
8. The KKK did this to Johnny with the letters KKK.
9. Esther thinks her mother took a train to this place.
10. Sara's dog that is killed by the Klan
11. Owns a shoe store in town
12. Leanora gets a signed book from her.
13. No one would help Leanora's family when they had a problem withthis.
14. ____ begins to have doubts about the Klan when they get more violent.
15. Does not approve of her husband's involvement with the Klan
16. Characteristic of Klan members

A=13	B=3	C=6	D=12
E=8	F=10	G=15	H=1
I=11	J=5	K=4	L=14
M=2	N=16	O=9	P=7

Witness Word Search 1

V	I	O	L	A	J	E	R	R	Y	F	I	E	L	D	W	B	K
L	F	R	A	N	K	S	L	E	O	P	O	L	D	D	A	R	R
E	Y	Y	I	L	N	J	J	C	H	O	F	E	A	R	G	I	H
W	S	N	T	R	K	J	E	B	I	I	I	C	R	Y	O	D	G
I	C	H	M	L	I	E	F	W	R	S	P	R	C	C	N	G	N
S	H	G	A	L	O	S	H	E	S	O	O	H	A	R	V	E	Y
C	O	B	R	T	R	T	A	K	H	N	O	L	R	O	O	Q	R
Y	O	X	R	T	E	H	V	R	B	N	R	M	Y	S	P	C	L
H	L	M	I	A	Y	E	G	O	A	K	B	H	S	S	E	N	K
K	O	V	E	J	N	R	Y	H	T	T	A	E	R	C	R	E	B
K	F	L	D	J	A	D	H	H	J	E	B	A	E	O	C	W	J
K	E	L	L	E	R	W	E	R	O	L	Y	V	E	L	E	S	T
T	F	B	V	O	D	T	X	D	H	T	H	E	V	L	L	P	Y
R	G	X	V	N	W	K	M	Z	N	K	E	N	E	E	L	A	S
A	S	M	U	R	D	E	R	P	N	H	H	L	S	G	E	P	B
I	S	U	T	T	E	R	E	G	Y	H	O	M	E	E	J	E	T
N	P	R	E	S	I	D	E	N	T	C	A	N	E	M	A	R	Y

Characteristic of Klan members (4)
Coolidge was elected as this. (9)
Does not approve of her husband's involvement with the Klan (5)
Esther is almost hit by one of these (5)
Esther thinks her mother took a train to this place. (6)
Group that harasses people in the town (3)
Group the Klan targets (4)
He gives Merlin the keys to his business. (7)
Holiday Esther enjoys celebrating (9)
Iris paid for her siblings to go there. (7)
Is a bootlegger on the side to earn extra money (4)
Johnny Reeves jumps off a ___________ because he is afraid of the Klan. (6)
Johnny says women are happiest at this place. (4)
Klan thinks this family is worse than the Sutters. (5)
Klansmen stole this from Merlin. (3)
Leanora gets a signed book from her. (6)
Leanora helps him and they become friends. (5)
Leopold and Loeb are charged with this. (6)
Mary struts around in these. (8)
Merlin runs away because he feels this. (4)
Merlin was supposed to put this in the Sutters' well. (6)
Mr. Field's weapon at the courhouse (4)
No one would help Leanora's family when they had a problem withthis. (5)
Owns a shoe store in town (3)
Percelle found one wrapped in a newspaper. (4)
Person in charge of maintaining peace in the town (8)
Place where Harvey and Klan do damage (5)
Place where Leanora is most often teased about being black (6)
Rich, white boy who was murdered (6)
Sale items that caused a stampede (6)
Sara never did this. (7)
Sara's dog that is killed by the Klan (5)
Saw the person who shot Ira Hirsh (6)
She is like a mother to Esther. (4)
She was stuck in a wagon in the cold for too long and later died: Mrs. ______. (6)
Shot Ira Hirsh (6)
Someone threw this through Sara's window. (4)
The KKK burns one on July 4th. (5)
The KKK did this to Johnny with the letters KKK. (7)
The Klan gives money to them. (4)
Wants to be married in KKK robes (4)
Was kicked out of the KKK (6)
Was suffocated by a sandbank cave-in (5)
What women got the right to do; Iris Weaver was excited to do this (4)
Where the town learns how Leanora rescued Esther (9)
____ begins to have doubts about the Klan when they get more violent. (6)
__________ and Loeb kill a teenage boy in Chicago. (7)

Witness Word Search 1 Answer Key

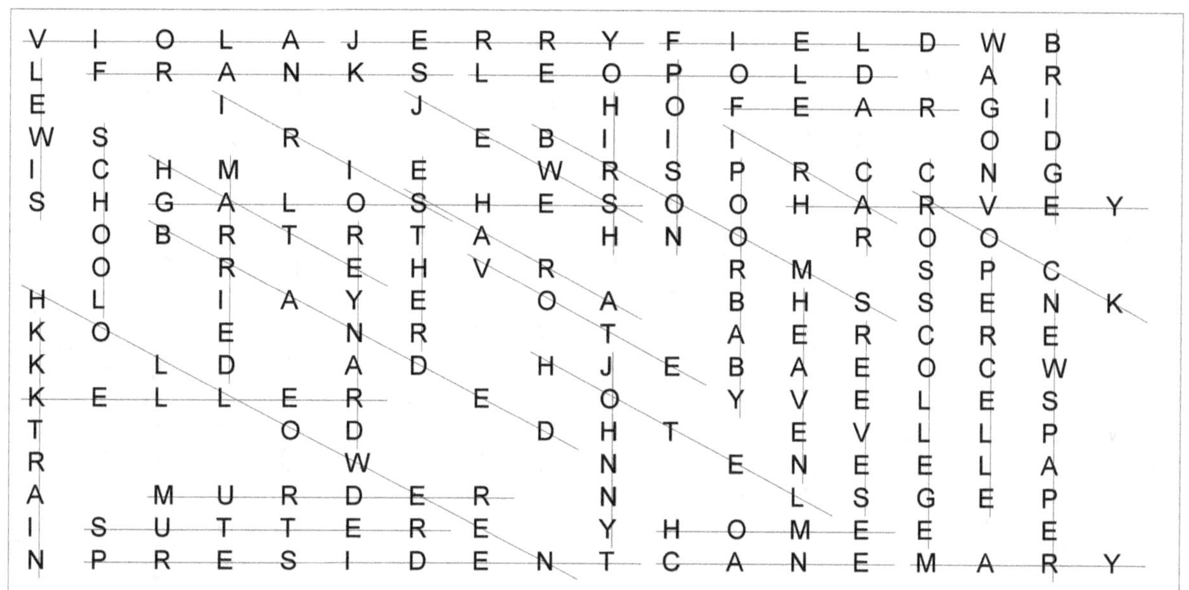

Characteristic of Klan members (4)
Coolidge was elected as this. (9)
Does not approve of her husband's involvement with the Klan (5)
Esther is almost hit by one of these (5)
Esther thinks her mother took a train to this place. (6)
Group that harasses people in the town (3)
Group the Klan targets (4)
He gives Merlin the keys to his business. (7)
Holiday Esther enjoys celebrating (9)
Iris paid for her siblings to go there. (7)
Is a bootlegger on the side to earn extra money (4)
Johnny Reeves jumps off a ___________ because he is afraid of the Klan. (6)
Johnny says women are happiest at this place. (4)
Klan thinks this family is worse than the Sutters. (5)
Klansmen stole this from Merlin. (3)
Leanora gets a signed book from her. (6)
Leanora helps him and they become friends. (5)
Leopold and Loeb are charged with this. (6)
Mary struts around in these. (8)
Merlin runs away because he feels this. (4)
Merlin was supposed to put this in the Sutters' well. (6)
Mr. Field's weapon at the courhouse (4)
No one would help Leanora's family when they had a problem withthis. (5)
Owns a shoe store in town (3)
Percelle found one wrapped in a newspaper. (4)
Person in charge of maintaining peace in the town (8)
Place where Harvey and Klan do damage (5)
Place where Leanora is most often teased about being black (6)
Rich, white boy who was murdered (6)
Sale items that caused a stampede (6)
Sara never did this. (7)
Sara's dog that is killed by the Klan (5)
Saw the person who shot Ira Hirsh (6)
She is like a mother to Esther. (4)
She was stuck in a wagon in the cold for too long and later died: Mrs. _____. (6)
Shot Ira Hirsh (6)
Someone threw this through Sara's window. (4)
The KKK burns one on July 4th. (5)
The KKK did this to Johnny with the letters KKK. (7)
The Klan gives money to them. (4)
Wants to be married in KKK robes (4)
Was kicked out of the KKK (6)
Was suffocated by a sandbank cave-in (5)
What women got the right to do; Iris Weaver was excited to do this (4)
Where the town learns how Leanora rescued Esther (9)
____ begins to have doubts about the Klan when they get more violent. (6)
__________ and Loeb kill a teenage boy in Chicago. (7)

Witness Word Search 2

G	L	B	K	W	Q	F	L	P	S	M	V	I	O	L	A	L	J
A	X	S	E	J	H	R	E	E	U	U	F	C	H	P	R	E	H
L	B	S	L	B	I	A	W	T	T	R	Y	X	O	E	E	O	B
O	R	X	L	K	R	N	I	T	T	D	C	V	T	R	E	P	V
S	I	M	E	F	S	K	S	I	E	E	F	O	E	C	V	O	X
H	D	G	R	P	H	S	R	B	R	R	M	I	L	E	E	L	T
E	G	P	O	I	S	O	N	O	M	Q	H	H	E	L	S	D	M
S	E	S	T	H	E	R	M	N	N	E	A	O	J	L	E	S	X
V	B	J	C	H	E	A	V	E	N	T	R	L	B	E	D	G	M
K	R	S	E	M	G	I	P	Y	K	R	V	L	F	F	R	C	E
V	O	Y	Y	W	H	R	T	H	K	A	E	O	I	E	C	R	S
R	O	C	K	J	S	A	R	A	K	I	Y	W	I	N	A	X	Y
F	M	T	G	O	C	D	T	B	H	N	Q	E	A	R	R	R	Z
L	S	H	E	H	H	C	M	E	A	G	J	E	M	G	I	N	M
P	O	O	R	N	O	R	A	D	V	B	B	N	C	R	O	S	S
L	V	Q	J	N	O	R	R	N	R	E	Y	N	A	R	D	N	N
T	G	L	P	Y	L	D	Y	N	E	W	S	P	A	P	E	R	Z

Characteristic of Klan members (4)
Does not approve of her husband's involvement with the Klan (5)
Esther is almost hit by one of these (5)
Esther thinks her mother took a train to this place. (6)
Group that harasses people in the town (3)
Group the Klan targets (4)
Hassles Leanora about her race (9)
He gives Merlin the keys to his business. (7)
Holiday Esther enjoys celebrating (9)
Iris paid for her siblings to go there. (7)
Is a bootlegger on the side to earn extra money (4)
Johnny Reeves jumps off a ___________ because he is afraid of the Klan. (6)
Johnny says women are happiest at this place. (4)
Klan thinks this family is worse than the Sutters. (5)
Klansmen stole this from Merlin. (3)
Leanora gets a signed book from her. (6)
Leanora helps him and they become friends. (5)
Leopold and Loeb are charged with this. (6)
Mary struts around in these. (8)
Merlin runs away because he feels this. (4)
Merlin was supposed to put this in the Sutters' well. (6)
Mr. Field's weapon at the courhouse (4)
No one would help Leanora's family when they had a problem withthis. (5)
Owns a shoe store in town (3)
Percelle found one wrapped in a newspaper. (4)
Person in charge of maintaining peace in the town (8)
Place where Harvey and Klan do damage (5)
Place where Leanora is most often teased about being black (6)
Rich, white boy who was murdered (6)
Sale items that caused a stampede (6)
Sara's dog that is killed by the Klan (5)
Saw the person who shot Ira Hirsh (6)
She is like a mother to Esther. (4)
She was stuck in a wagon in the cold for too long and later died: Mrs. ______. (6)
Shot Ira Hirsh (6)
Someone threw this through Sara's window. (4)
The KKK burns one on July 4th. (5)
The Klan gives money to them. (4)
Tries to rescue his girlfriend from the orphanage (6)
Wants to be married in KKK robes (4)
Was kicked out of the KKK (6)
Was suffocated by a sandbank cave-in (5)
What women got the right to do; Iris Weaver was excited to do this (4)
Where the town learns how Leanora rescued Esther (9)
____ begins to have doubts about the Klan when they get more violent. (6)
__________ and Loeb kill a teenage boy in Chicago. (7)

Witness Word Search 2 Answer Key

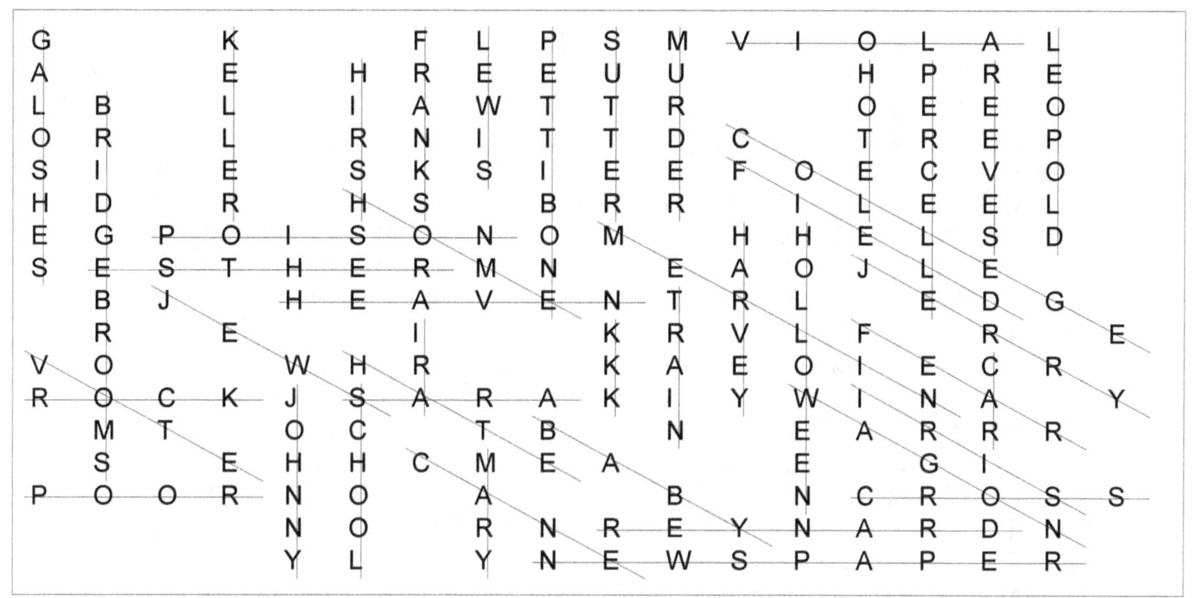

Characteristic of Klan members (4)
Does not approve of her husband's involvement with the Klan (5)
Esther is almost hit by one of these (5)
Esther thinks her mother took a train to this place. (6)
Group that harasses people in the town (3)
Group the Klan targets (4)
Hassles Leanora about her race (9)
He gives Merlin the keys to his business. (7)
Holiday Esther enjoys celebrating (9)
Iris paid for her siblings to go there. (7)
Is a bootlegger on the side to earn extra money (4)
Johnny Reeves jumps off a ___________ because he is afraid of the Klan. (6)
Johnny says women are happiest at this place. (4)
Klan thinks this family is worse than the Sutters. (5)
Klansmen stole this from Merlin. (3)
Leanora gets a signed book from her. (6)
Leanora helps him and they become friends. (5)
Leopold and Loeb are charged with this. (6)
Mary struts around in these. (8)
Merlin runs away because he feels this. (4)
Merlin was supposed to put this in the Sutters' well. (6)
Mr. Field's weapon at the courhouse (4)
No one would help Leanora's family when they had a problem withthis. (5)
Owns a shoe store in town (3)
Percelle found one wrapped in a newspaper. (4)
Person in charge of maintaining peace in the town (8)
Place where Harvey and Klan do damage (5)
Place where Leanora is most often teased about being black (6)
Rich, white boy who was murdered (6)
Sale items that caused a stampede (6)
Sara's dog that is killed by the Klan (5)
Saw the person who shot Ira Hirsh (6)
She is like a mother to Esther. (4)
She was stuck in a wagon in the cold for too long and later died: Mrs. _____. (6)
Shot Ira Hirsh (6)
Someone threw this through Sara's window. (4)
The KKK burns one on July 4th. (5)
The Klan gives money to them. (4)
Tries to rescue his girlfriend from the orphanage (6)
Wants to be married in KKK robes (4)
Was kicked out of the KKK (6)
Was suffocated by a sandbank cave-in (5)
What women got the right to do; Iris Weaver was excited to do this (4)
Where the town learns how Leanora rescued Esther (9)
____ begins to have doubts about the Klan when they get more violent. (6)
__________ and Loeb kill a teenage boy in Chicago. (7)

Wine Word Search 3

R	E	E	V	E	S	V	O	T	E	P	R	E	S	I	D	E	N	T	Q
P	C	S	B	I	L	D	C	Y	G	O	O	K	Q	R	F	K	M	W	V
E	K	T	R	L	O	N	F	S	A	I	H	O	H	I	I	E	X	S	N
R	K	H	I	E	B	L	E	W	L	S	J	E	R	S	E	L	Y	C	T
C	K	E	D	W	N	J	A	A	O	O	H	G	A	B	L	L	F	H	K
E	M	R	G	I	P	E	R	G	S	N	H	Z	D	V	D	E	I	O	H
L	H	L	E	S	E	R	S	O	H	B	O	Y	R	C	E	R	T	O	L
L	L	O	R	N	T	R	T	N	E	F	L	S	A	R	A	N	Z	L	G
E	E	T	M	K	T	Y	H	H	S	Y	L	D	M	J	W	N	G	E	F
R	A	B	J	E	I	T	Q	A	L	C	O	L	L	E	G	E	E	O	N
Y	N	H	R	N	B	M	R	F	R	G	W	B	M	R	M	V	R	P	S
R	O	K	A	A	O	U	N	A	R	V	E	A	I	A	B	R	A	O	V
R	R	S	D	T	N	R	J	Q	I	A	E	B	R	H	R	E	L	L	V
C	A	R	U	T	E	D	J	O	H	N	N	Y	A	O	O	Y	D	D	Q
R	T	O	D	T	Q	E	E	R	X	I	T	K	T	T	O	N	J	R	J
O	N	C	T	T	T	R	S	D	T	W	R	B	S	E	M	A	E	M	Y
S	K	K	T	N	M	E	R	L	I	N	M	S	C	L	S	R	W	B	J
S	J	Z	H	M	M	A	R	R	I	E	D	W	H	R	Y	D	S	S	C

BABY	FIELD	HOTEL	LEWIS	REEVES
BRANDED	FITZGERALD	IRA	MARRIED	REYNARD
BRIDGE	FRANKS	IRIS	MARY	ROCK
BROOMS	GALOSHES	JERRY	MERLIN	SARA
CANE	HARVEY	JEWS	MURDER	SCHOOL
CAR	HATE	JOHNNY	PERCELLE	SUTTER
COLLEGE	HEAVEN	KELLER	PETTIBONE	TRAIN
CROSS	HIRSH	KKK	POISON	VIOLA
ESTHER	HOLLOWEEN	LEANORA	POOR	VOTE
FEAR	HOME	LEOPOLD	PRESIDENT	WAGON

Wine Word Search 3 Answer Key

```
R E E V E S V O T E P R E S I D E N T
P   S B I         G O O     R F K    
E K T R L O   F   A I H O   I I E   S
R K H I E   L E W L S   E R S E L   C
C K E D W   J A A O O     A   L L F H
E   R G I P E R G S N H     V D E I O
L H   E S E R   O H   O     C E R T O
L L O     T R   N E   L S A R A N Z L
E E   M   T Y H   S   L         N G E
  A B   E I T   A   C O L L E G E E O
  N H R   B M R F R   W B M       R P
  O   A A O U   A R V E A I A B R A O
  R S   T N R     I A E B R H R E L L
C A R U   E D J O H N N Y A O O Y D D
R   O   T   E E     I   K   T O N J  
O   C     T R   D     R   S E M A E  
S   K     M E R L I N   S   L S R W  
S         M A R R I E D   H     D S  
```

BABY
BRANDED
BRIDGE
BROOMS
CANE
CAR
COLLEGE
CROSS
ESTHER
FEAR

FIELD
FITZGERALD
FRANKS
GALOSHES
HARVEY
HATE
HEAVEN
HIRSH
HOLLOWEEN
HOME

HOTEL
IRA
IRIS
JERRY
JEWS
JOHNNY
KELLER
KKK
LEANORA
LEOPOLD

LEWIS
MARRIED
MARY
MERLIN
MURDER
PERCELLE
PETTIBONE
POISON
POOR
PRESIDENT

REEVES
REYNARD
ROCK
SARA
SCHOOL
SUTTER
TRAIN
VIOLA
VOTE
WAGON

Wine Word Search 4

```
S J P W G F R A N K S P J P B C R O S S
H B O M X E Q N S E I R E E G A A N D L
M A O H C A V F C L K D L R W R B N K H
S A R A N R Z W H L L K N J C S H Y E Y
M P R V Y N C H O E F B W A E E L O G T
J X B Y E S Y O O R A K Y P P R L T M C
B B G R Q Y H X L T F V K W H P R L R E
P R E S I D E N T L E I E K A N I Y E T
M A O W K D X K F E E L E N T E R N M F
A N K O C P G Y P W X G P L E W I H G F
R D J L M C O E N I E G E F D S S O R W
R E E V E S H I R S H S L E O P O L D X
I D K Q O A P R S O U Y T V J A M L Q M
E L W X L T N A V O C T Z H B P U O K F
D W A G O N E O C M N K T W E E R W Q Z
M E R L I N P T R A I N N E F R D E W V
P J F I T Z G E R A L D X J R B E E D B
G A L O S H E S V I O L A R F D R N C P
```

BABY
BRANDED
BRIDGE
BROOMS
CANE
CAR
COLLEGE
CROSS
ESTHER
FEAR
FIELD
FITZGERALD
FRANKS
GALOSHES
HARVEY
HATE
HEAVEN
HIRSH
HOLLOWEEN
HOME
HOTEL
IRA
IRIS
JERRY
JEWS
JOHNNY
KELLER
KIDNAPPING
KKK
LEANORA
LEOPOLD
LEWIS
MARRIED
MARY
MERLIN
MURDER
NEWSPAPER
PERCELLE
POISON
POOR
PRESIDENT
REEVES
ROCK
SARA
SCHOOL
SUTTER
TRAIN
VIOLA
VOTE
WAGON

Wine Word Search 4 Answer Key

	J	P			F	R	A	N	K	S	P	J		B	C	R	O	S	S
H		O			E			S	E	I		E	E		A	A			
M	A	O	H		A			C	L		D		R	W	R	B	N		
S	A	R	A	N	R			H	L			N	J	C	S	H	Y	E	
		R	V		N	C	H	O	E				A	E	E		O		
		B	Y	E		Y	O	O	R	A	K			P	R	L		M	
B	B		R		Y			L	T	F	V	K		H	P	R	L		E
P	R	E	S	I	D	E	N	T	L	E	I	E	K	A	N	I	Y	E	
M	A	O			D				E	E	L	E	N	T	E	R	N		
A	N		O		P	G			W		G		L	E	W	I	H	G	
R	D		L	M		O	E		I	E		E		D	S	S	O		
R	E	E	V	E	S	H	I	R	S	H	S	L	E	O	P	O	L	D	
I	D			O	A		R	S	O	U		T			A	M	L		
E					T	N	A		O	C	T		H		P	U	O		
D	W	A	G	O	N	E	O			N	K	T		E	E	R	W		
M	E	R	L	I	N		T	R	A	I	N		E		R	D	E		
		F	I	T	Z	G	E	R	A	L	D			R		E	E		
G	A	L	O	S	H	E	S	V	I	O	L	A				R	N		

BABY	FIELD	HOTEL	LEOPOLD	PRESIDENT
BRANDED	FITZGERALD	IRA	LEWIS	REEVES
BRIDGE	FRANKS	IRIS	MARRIED	ROCK
BROOMS	GALOSHES	JERRY	MARY	SARA
CANE	HARVEY	JEWS	MERLIN	SCHOOL
CAR	HATE	JOHNNY	MURDER	SUTTER
COLLEGE	HEAVEN	KELLER	NEWSPAPER	TRAIN
CROSS	HIRSH	KIDNAPPING	PERCELLE	VIOLA
ESTHER	HOLLOWEEN	KKK	POISON	VOTE
FEAR	HOME	LEANORA	POOR	WAGON

Witness Crossword 1

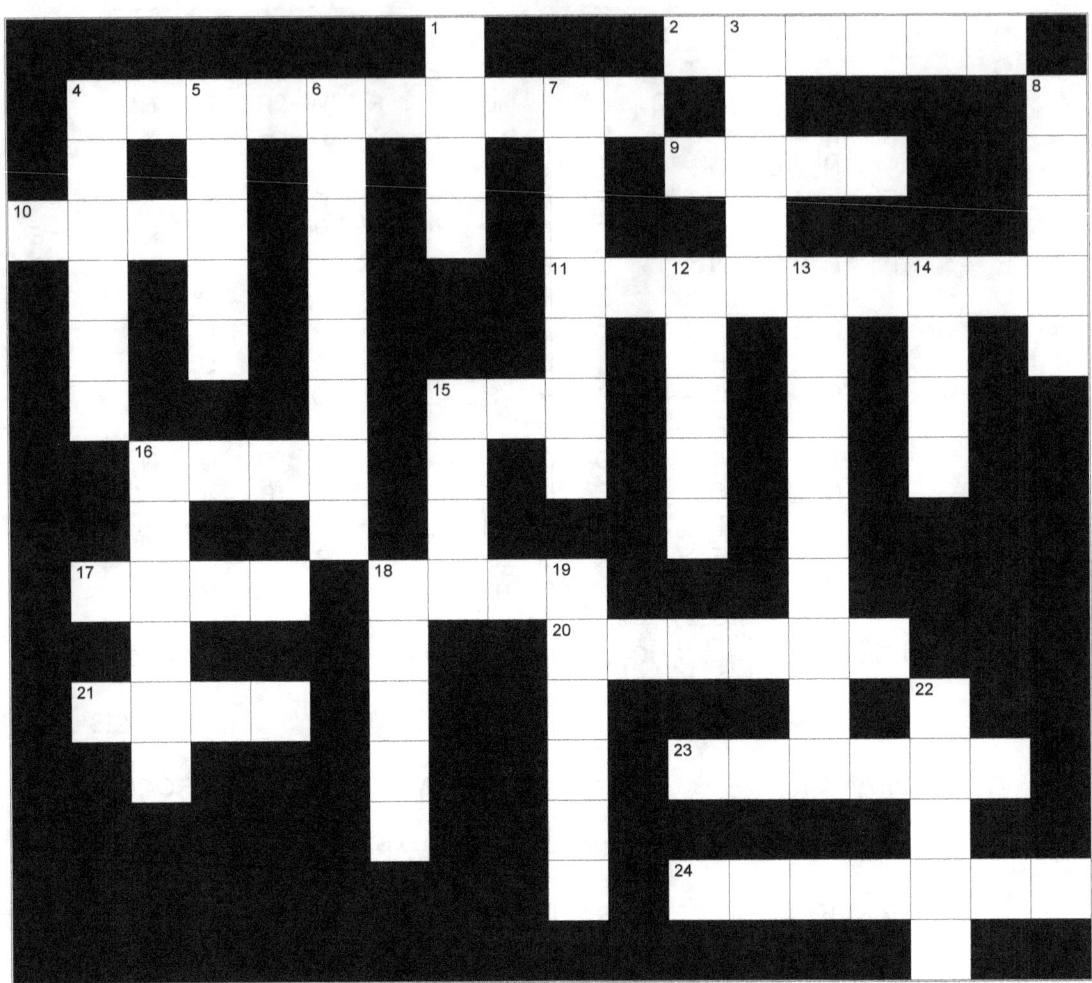

Across
2. Place where Leanora is most often teased about being black
4. Helps save Ira Hirsh
9. What women got the right to do; Iris Weaver was excited to do this
10. She is like a mother to Esther.
11. Where the town learns how Leanora rescued Esther
15. Klansmen stole this from Merlin.
16. Johnny says women are happiest at this place.
17. Percelle found one wrapped in a newspaper.
18. Merlin runs away because he feels this.
20. Saw the person who shot Ira Hirsh
21. Group the Klan targets
23. She was stuck in a wagon in the cold for too long and later died: Mrs. _____.
24. Sara never did this.

.

Down
1. Is a bootlegger on the side to earn extra money
3. The KKK burns one on July 4th.
4. Rich, white boy who was murdered
5. Esther is almost hit by one of these
6. Mary struts around in these.
7. Clears Merlin's name
8. Sara's dog that is killed by the Klan
12. No one would help Leanora's family when they had a problem withthis.
13. Coolidge was elected as this.
14. The Klan gives money to them.
15. Mr. Field's weapon at the courhouse
16. Esther thinks her mother took a train to this place.
18. Leanora helps him and they become friends.
19. Was kicked out of the KKK
22. Was suffocated by a sandbank cave-in

Witness Crossword 1 Answer Key

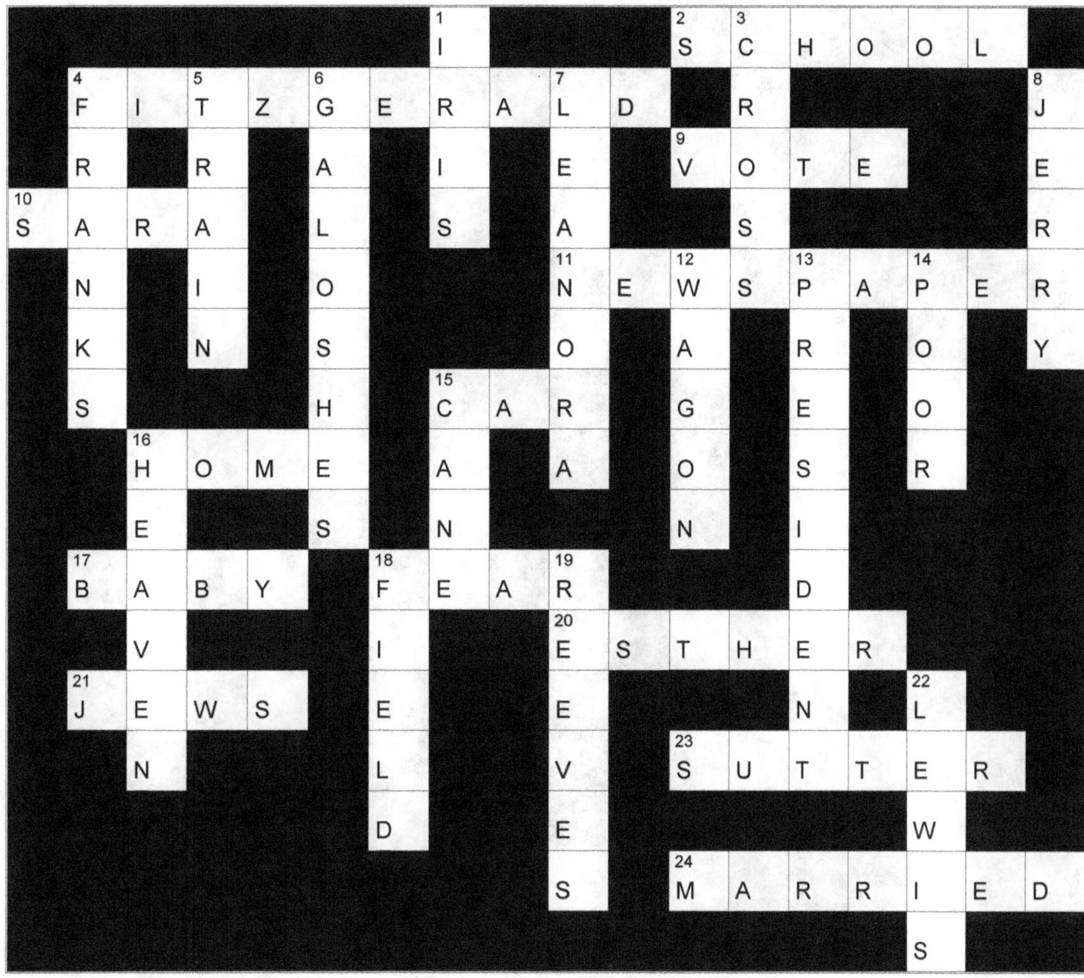

Across

2. Place where Leanora is most often teased about being black
4. Helps save Ira Hirsh
9. What women got the right to do; Iris Weaver was excited to do this
10. She is like a mother to Esther.
11. Where the town learns how Leanora rescued Esther
15. Klansmen stole this from Merlin.
16. Johnny says women are happiest at this place.
17. Percelle found one wrapped in a newspaper.
18. Merlin runs away because he feels this.
20. Saw the person who shot Ira Hirsh
21. Group the Klan targets
23. She was stuck in a wagon in the cold for too long and later died: Mrs. _____.
24. Sara never did this.

.

Down

1. Is a bootlegger on the side to earn extra money
3. The KKK burns one on July 4th.
4. Rich, white boy who was murdered
5. Esther is almost hit by one of these
6. Mary struts around in these.
7. Clears Merlin's name
8. Sara's dog that is killed by the Klan
12. No one would help Leanora's family when they had a problem withthis.
13. Coolidge was elected as this.
14. The Klan gives money to them.
15. Mr. Field's weapon at the courhouse
16. Esther thinks her mother took a train to this place.
18. Leanora helps him and they become friends.
19. Was kicked out of the KKK
22. Was suffocated by a sandbank cave-in

Witness Crossword 2

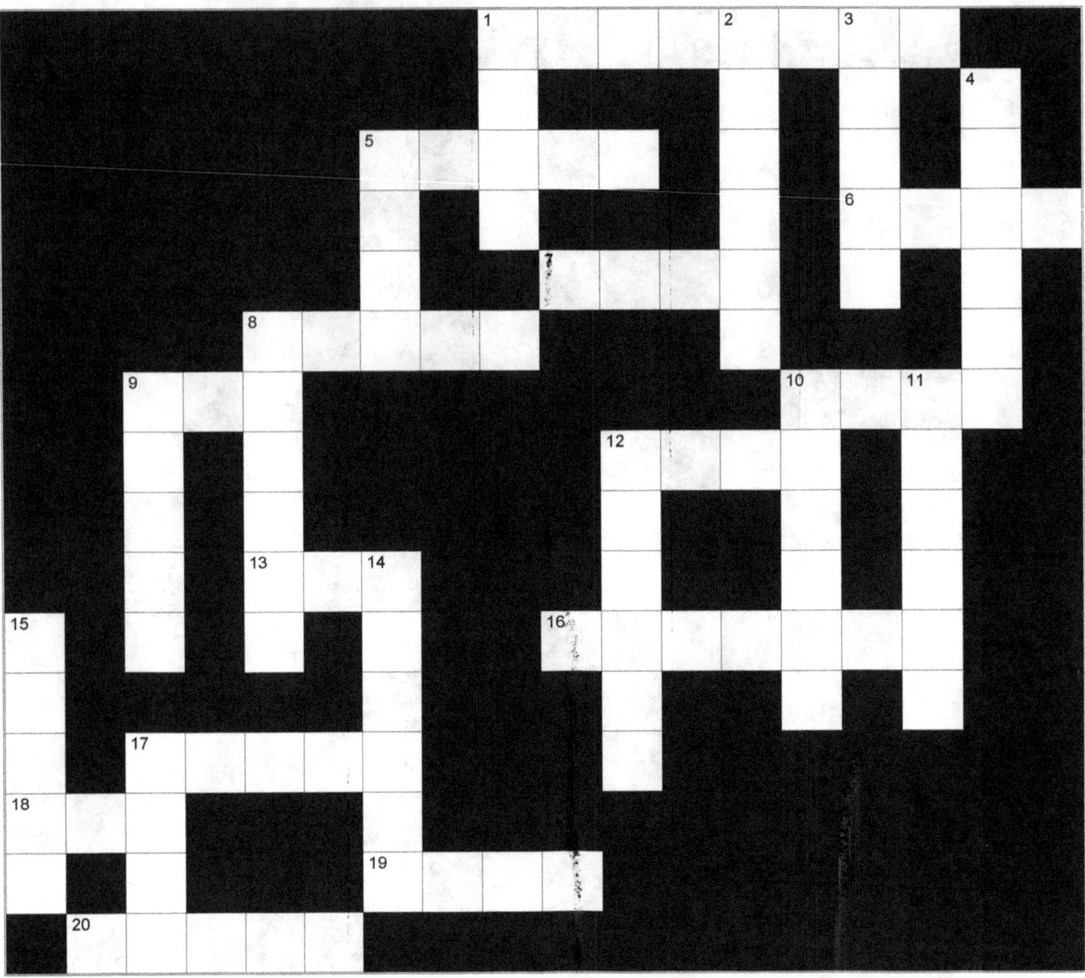

Across

1. Person in charge of maintaining peace in the town
5. Does not approve of her husband's involvement with the Klan
6. Is a bootlegger on the side to earn extra money
7. Mr. Field's weapon at the courhouse
8. Leanora helps him and they become friends.
9. Klansmen stole this from Merlin.
10. Johnny says women are happiest at this place.
12. She is like a mother to Esther.
13. Group that harasses people in the town
16. Iris paid for her siblings to go there.
17. Place where Harvey and Klan do damage
18. Owns a shoe store in town
19. Someone threw this through Sara's window.
20. Sara's dog that is killed by the Klan

Down

1. The Klan gives money to them.
2. Saw the person who shot Ira Hirsh
3. Was suffocated by a sandbank cave-in
4. Johnny Reeves jumps off a ___________ because he is afraid of the Klan.
5. What women got the right to do; Iris Weaver was excited to do this
8. Rich, white boy who was murdered
9. The KKK burns one on July 4th.
10. ____ begins to have doubts about the Klan when they get more violent.
11. Leopold and Loeb are charged with this.
12. Place where Leanora is most often teased about being black
14. Leanora gets a signed book from her.
15. Esther is almost hit by one of these
17. Characteristic of Klan members

Witness Crossword 2 Answer Key

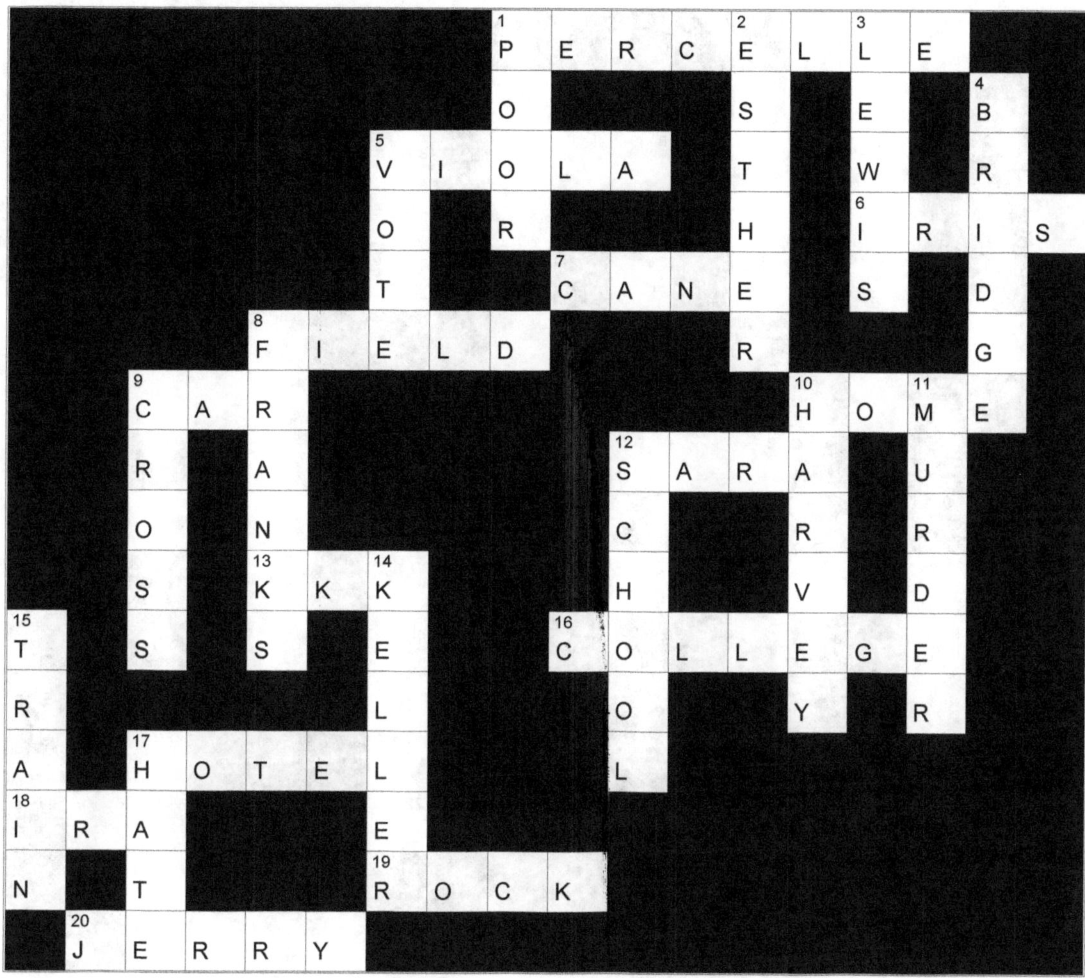

Across

1. Person in charge of maintaining peace in the town
5. Does not approve of her husband's involvement with the Klan
6. Is a bootlegger on the side to earn extra money
7. Mr. Field's weapon at the courhouse
8. Leanora helps him and they become friends.
9. Klansmen stole this from Merlin.
10. Johnny says women are happiest at this place.
12. She is like a mother to Esther.
13. Group that harasses people in the town
16. Iris paid for her siblings to go there.
17. Place where Harvey and Klan do damage
18. Owns a shoe store in town
19. Someone threw this through Sara's window.
20. Sara's dog that is killed by the Klan

Down

1. The Klan gives money to them.
2. Saw the person who shot Ira Hirsh
3. Was suffocated by a sandbank cave-in
4. Johnny Reeves jumps off a ___________ because he is afraid of the Klan.
5. What women got the right to do; Iris Weaver was excited to do this
8. Rich, white boy who was murdered
9. The KKK burns one on July 4th.
10. ____ begins to have doubts about the Klan when they get more violent.
11. Leopold and Loeb are charged with this.
12. Place where Leanora is most often teased about being black
14. Leanora gets a signed book from her.
15. Esther is almost hit by one of these
17. Characteristic of Klan members

Witness Crossword 3

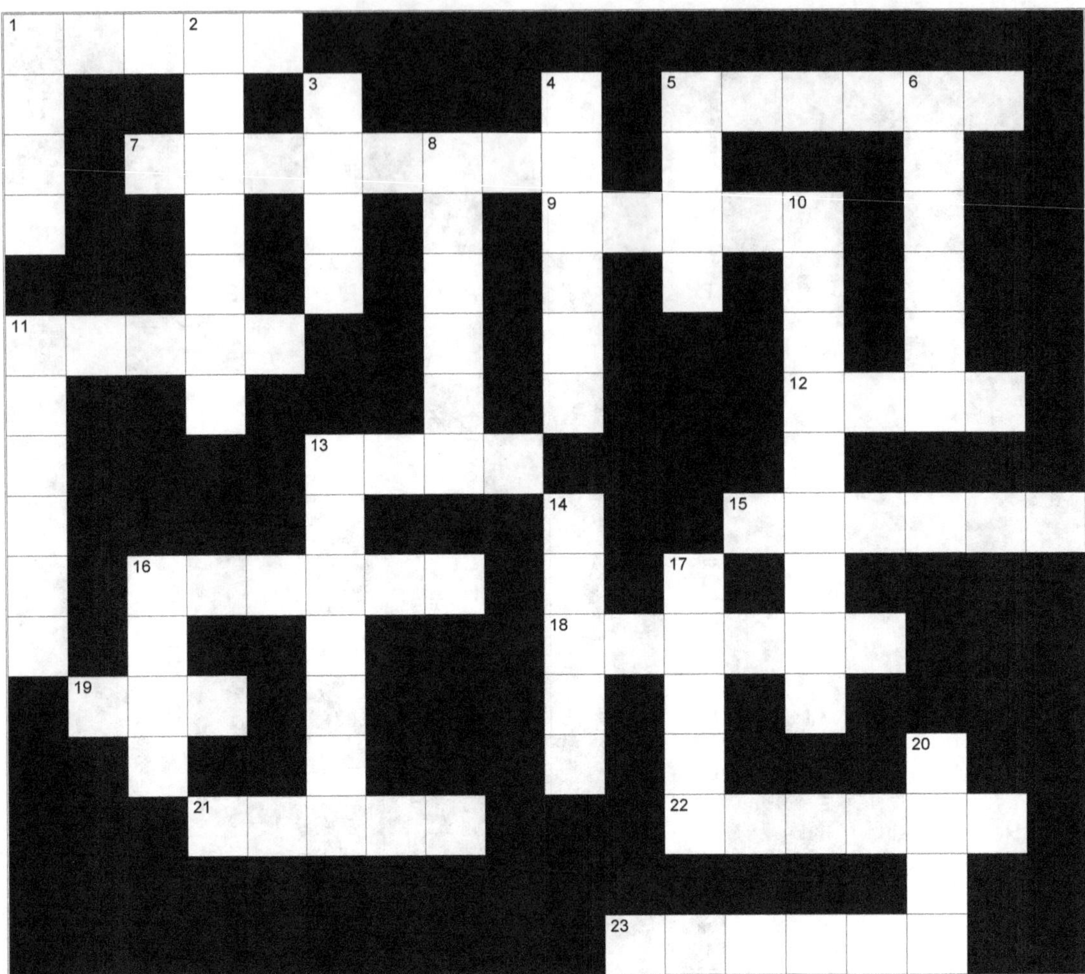

Across

1. Does not approve of her husband's involvement with the Klan
5. Rich, white boy who was murdered
7. Mary struts around in these.
9. Esther is almost hit by one of these
11. Sara's dog that is killed by the Klan
12. She is like a mother to Esther.
13. Mr. Field's weapon at the courhouse
15. ____ begins to have doubts about the Klan when they get more violent.
16. Tries to rescue his girlfriend from the orphanage
18. Was kicked out of the KKK
19. Owns a shoe store in town
21. Leanora helps him and they become friends.
22. She was stuck in a wagon in the cold for too long and later died: Mrs. _____.
23. Sale items that caused a stampede

Down

1. What women got the right to do; Iris Weaver was excited to do this
2. Clears Merlin's name
3. Someone threw this through Sara's window.
4. Saw the person who shot Ira Hirsh
5. Merlin runs away because he feels this.
6. Leanora gets a signed book from her.
8. Esther thinks her mother took a train to this place.
10. Where the town learns how Leanora rescued Esther
11. Shot Ira Hirsh
13. Iris paid for her siblings to go there.
14. Klan thinks this family is worse than the Sutters.
16. Wants to be married in KKK robes
17. Was suffocated by a sandbank cave-in
20. Group the Klan targets

Witness Crossword 3 Answer Key

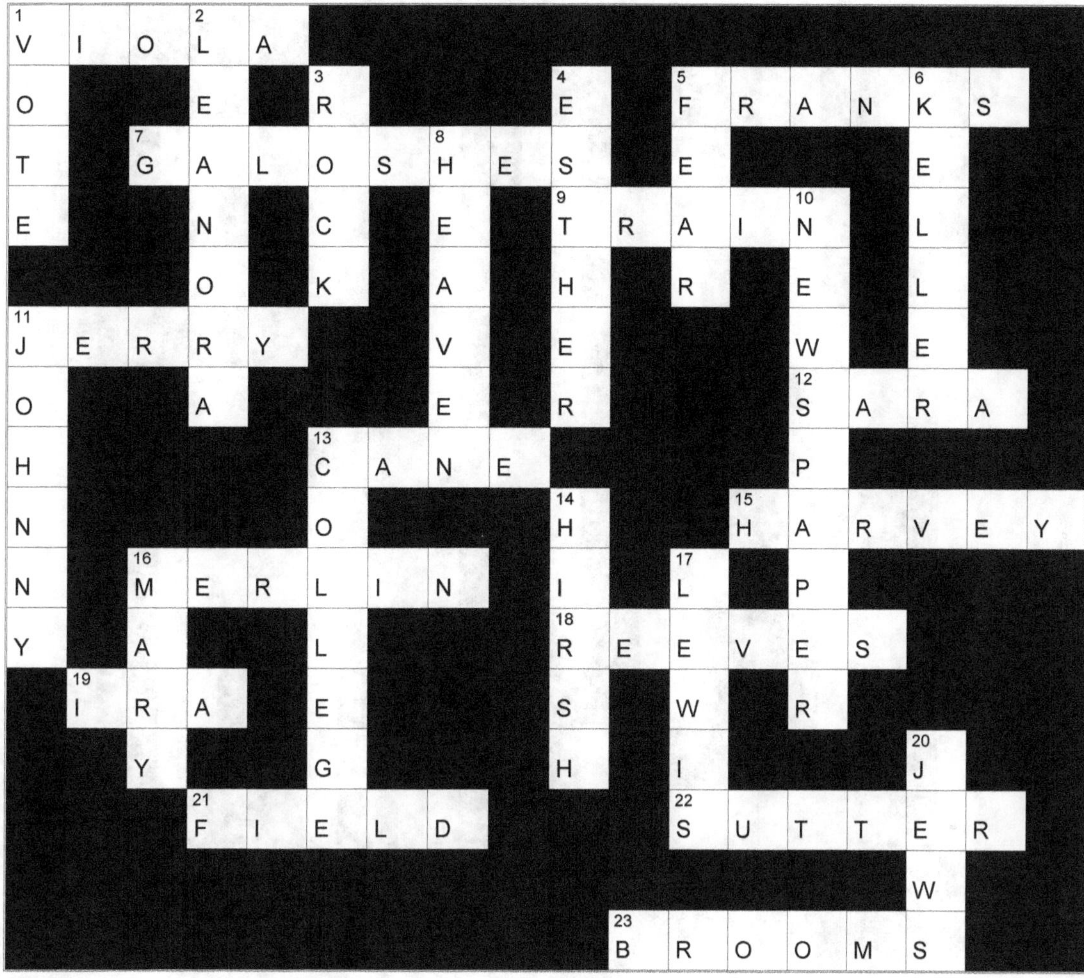

Across

1. Does not approve of her husband's involvement with the Klan
5. Rich, white boy who was murdered
7. Mary struts around in these.
9. Esther is almost hit by one of these
11. Sara's dog that is killed by the Klan
12. She is like a mother to Esther.
13. Mr. Field's weapon at the courhouse
15. _____ begins to have doubts about the Klan when they get more violent.
16. Tries to rescue his girlfriend from the orphanage
18. Was kicked out of the KKK
19. Owns a shoe store in town
21. Leanora helps him and they become friends.
22. She was stuck in a wagon in the cold for too long and later died: Mrs. _____.
23. Sale items that caused a stampede

Down

1. What women got the right to do; Iris Weaver was excited to do this
2. Clears Merlin's name
3. Someone threw this through Sara's window.
4. Saw the person who shot Ira Hirsh
5. Merlin runs away because he feels this.
6. Leanora gets a signed book from her.
8. Esther thinks her mother took a train to this place.
10. Where the town learns how Leanora rescued Esther
11. Shot Ira Hirsh
13. Iris paid for her siblings to go there.
14. Klan thinks this family is worse than the Sutters.
16. Wants to be married in KKK robes
17. Was suffocated by a sandbank cave-in
20. Group the Klan targets

Witness Crossword 4

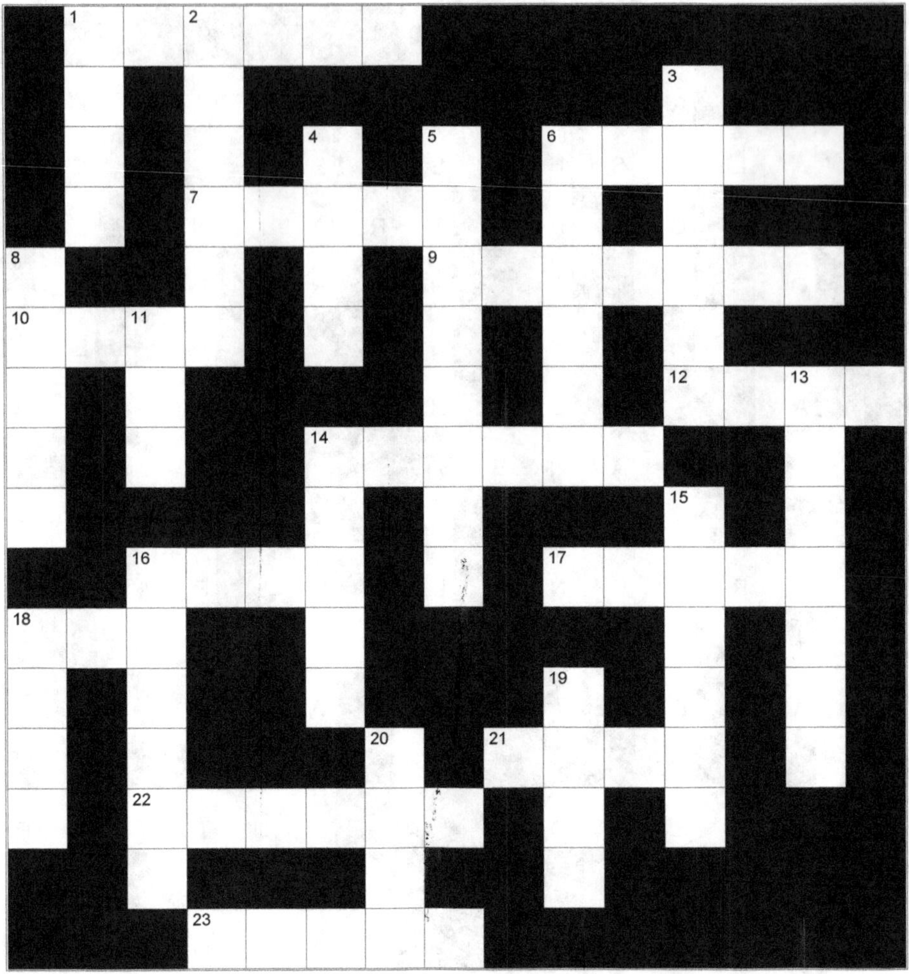

Across

1. Tries to rescue his girlfriend from the orphanage
6. Klan thinks this family is worse than the Sutters.
7. Does not approve of her husband's involvement with the Klan
9. Clears Merlin's name
10. Is a bootlegger on the side to earn extra money
12. She is like a mother to Esther.
14. Shot Ira Hirsh
16. Merlin runs away because he feels this.
17. Esther is almost hit by one of these
18. Klansmen stole this from Merlin.
21. What women got the right to do; Iris Weaver was excited to do this
22. Leanora gets a signed book from her.
23. The KKK burns one on July 4th.

Down

1. Wants to be married in KKK robes
2. Was kicked out of the KKK
3. Sale items that caused a stampede
4. Someone threw this through Sara's window.
5. Mary struts around in these.
6. Esther thinks her mother took a train to this place.
8. Leanora helps him and they become friends.
11. Owns a shoe store in town
13. He gives Merlin the keys to his business.
14. Sara's dog that is killed by the Klan
15. ____ begins to have doubts about the Klan when they get more violent.
16. Rich, white boy who was murdered
18. Mr. Field's weapon at the courhouse
19. The Klan gives money to them.
20. Group the Klan targets

Witness Crossword 4 Answer Key

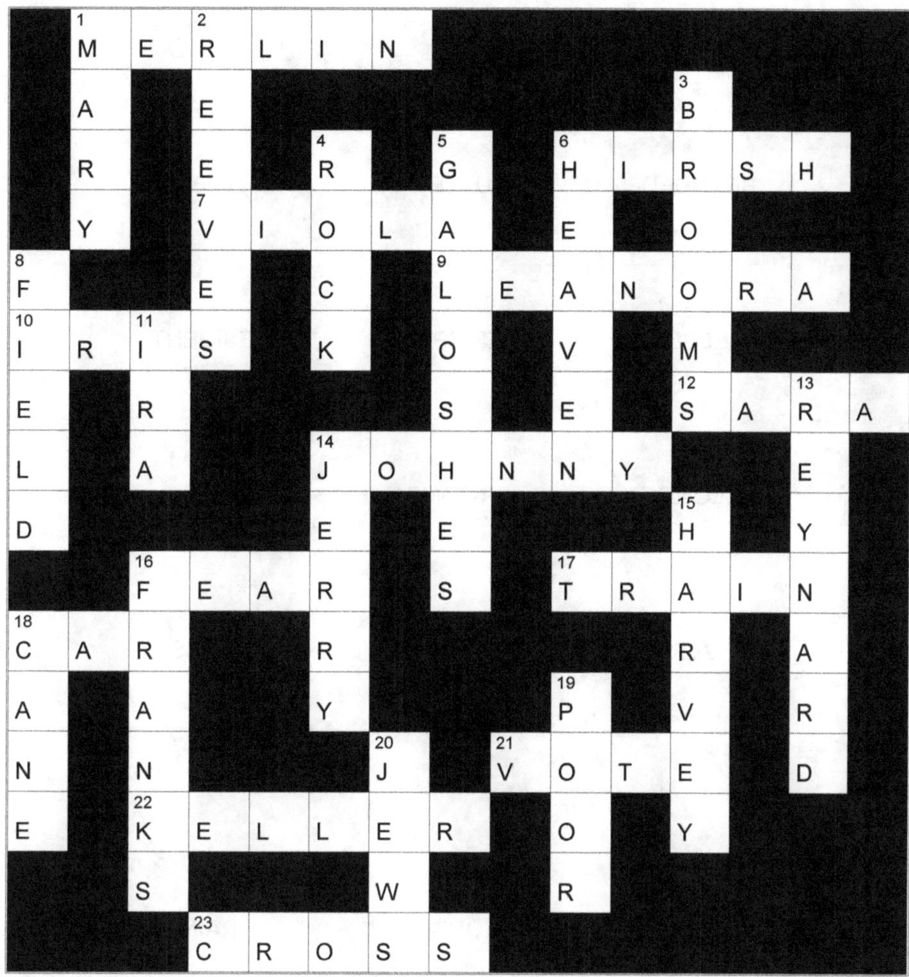

Across
1. Tries to rescue his girlfriend from the orphanage
6. Klan thinks this family is worse than the Sutters.
7. Does not approve of her husband's involvement with the Klan
9. Clears Merlin's name
10. Is a bootlegger on the side to earn extra money
12. She is like a mother to Esther.
14. Shot Ira Hirsh
16. Merlin runs away because he feels this.
17. Esther is almost hit by one of these
18. Klansmen stole this from Merlin.
21. What women got the right to do; Iris Weaver was excited to do this
22. Leanora gets a signed book from her.
23. The KKK burns one on July 4th.

Down
1. Wants to be married in KKK robes
2. Was kicked out of the KKK
3. Sale items that caused a stampede
4. Someone threw this through Sara's window.
5. Mary struts around in these.
6. Esther thinks her mother took a train to this place.
8. Leanora helps him and they become friends.
11. Owns a shoe store in town
13. He gives Merlin the keys to his business.
14. Sara's dog that is killed by the Klan
15. ____ begins to have doubts about the Klan when they get more violent.
16. Rich, white boy who was murdered
18. Mr. Field's weapon at the courhouse
19. The Klan gives money to them.
20. Group the Klan targets

LEANORA	CROSS	REYNARD	POOR	KIDNAPPING
LEWIS	BRANDED	SUTTER	KELLER	CANE
JOHNNY	REEVES	FREE SPACE	PRESIDENT	BABY
HATE	HOLLOWEEN	BROOMS	HOME	VOTE
SARA	FITZGERALD	ROCK	FRANKS	VIOLA

MERLIN	JERRY	LEOPOLD	TRAIN	NEWSPAPER
KKK	PERCELLE	HARVEY	MURDER	COLLEGE
FEAR	PETTIBONE	FREE SPACE	SCHOOL	HIRSH
FIELD	MARY	ESTHER	WAGON	MARRIED
IRA	IRIS	BRIDGE	HOTEL	JEWS

PETTIBONE	PRESIDENT	COLLEGE	LEANORA	BROOMS
KIDNAPPING	ESTHER	HATE	CANE	HOLLOWEEN
JOHNNY	BABY	FREE SPACE	KKK	BRANDED
POISON	JERRY	MERLIN	GALOSHES	HEAVEN
MARY	HOTEL	LEOPOLD	CAR	SARA

HOME	ROCK	SUTTER	POOR	KELLER
MARRIED	CROSS	FITZGERALD	VOTE	TRAIN
FRANKS	WAGON	FREE SPACE	PERCELLE	HIRSH
FEAR	JEWS	REEVES	REYNARD	SCHOOL
IRA	VIOLA	IRIS	FIELD	MURDER

KKK	MARY	POISON	VIOLA	HEAVEN
PERCELLE	HATE	MURDER	IRIS	LEWIS
PETTIBONE	REYNARD	FREE SPACE	KELLER	CROSS
FITZGERALD	FEAR	HOTEL	BRANDED	PRESIDENT
FRANKS	REEVES	KIDNAPPING	JOHNNY	SCHOOL

SARA	ESTHER	COLLEGE	MERLIN	LEOPOLD
CANE	BABY	BRIDGE	FIELD	POOR
SUTTER	VOTE	FREE SPACE	WAGON	NEWSPAPER
CAR	TRAIN	LEANORA	ROCK	JERRY
HOME	GALOSHES	BROOMS	JEWS	HARVEY

SARA	BROOMS	MURDER	GALOSHES	POOR
FEAR	IRIS	MERLIN	FIELD	PETTIBONE
HARVEY	BABY	FREE SPACE	CROSS	CANE
KKK	HOME	BRANDED	PRESIDENT	BRIDGE
REEVES	MARY	FITZGERALD	HATE	REYNARD

LEOPOLD	TRAIN	JEWS	NEWSPAPER	POISON
VIOLA	FRANKS	SUTTER	HOLLOWEEN	KELLER
SCHOOL	MARRIED	FREE SPACE	VOTE	CAR
LEANORA	HIRSH	IRA	ESTHER	PERCELLE
KIDNAPPING	JERRY	COLLEGE	ROCK	HOTEL

MARRIED	FIELD	PRESIDENT	JOHNNY	TRAIN
HOTEL	NEWSPAPER	JEWS	HOME	LEOPOLD
SCHOOL	HOLLOWEEN	FREE SPACE	SARA	FITZGERALD
BABY	JERRY	POISON	PETTIBONE	IRA
LEWIS	HARVEY	KIDNAPPING	SUTTER	MURDER

FEAR	BRANDED	PERCELLE	KKK	MERLIN
REYNARD	CROSS	FRANKS	CAR	HIRSH
HEAVEN	WAGON	FREE SPACE	LEANORA	COLLEGE
POOR	VOTE	GALOSHES	BROOMS	ESTHER
KELLER	IRIS	VIOLA	HATE	MARY

IRIS	TRAIN	LEOPOLD	IRA	KKK
CAR	MARY	PETTIBONE	HIRSH	HARVEY
SUTTER	BABY	FREE SPACE	BRANDED	FITZGERALD
BROOMS	WAGON	POOR	NEWSPAPER	REEVES
CANE	PERCELLE	ESTHER	ROCK	SARA

JEWS	FRANKS	MERLIN	HOLLOWEEN	MARRIED
PRESIDENT	CROSS	SCHOOL	BRIDGE	HOME
KIDNAPPING	FIELD	FREE SPACE	GALOSHES	HATE
LEWIS	FEAR	LEANORA	HEAVEN	JERRY
JOHNNY	VIOLA	REYNARD	HOTEL	KELLER

MARRIED	PRESIDENT	CROSS	VOTE	ESTHER
GALOSHES	LEOPOLD	KKK	HOME	CANE
JERRY	JEWS	FREE SPACE	FEAR	CAR
REYNARD	HATE	TRAIN	BROOMS	JOHNNY
POISON	SUTTER	COLLEGE	KELLER	LEWIS

BRIDGE	HARVEY	IRIS	HOTEL	NEWSPAPER
FITZGERALD	HIRSH	IRA	PETTIBONE	HEAVEN
BRANDED	SCHOOL	FREE SPACE	LEANORA	VIOLA
PERCELLE	WAGON	KIDNAPPING	BABY	SARA
FIELD	MURDER	MERLIN	REEVES	MARY

MARRIED	IRA	MARY	GALOSHES	HATE
HOTEL	LEWIS	BABY	KELLER	LEANORA
CROSS	HIRSH	FREE SPACE	KKK	POOR
KIDNAPPING	CANE	JERRY	FRANKS	BROOMS
MERLIN	COLLEGE	BRIDGE	HEAVEN	ROCK

SARA	REEVES	LEOPOLD	VIOLA	IRIS
HOLLOWEEN	HARVEY	NEWSPAPER	CAR	ESTHER
FITZGERALD	PERCELLE	FREE SPACE	JEWS	PETTIBONE
VOTE	BRANDED	REYNARD	TRAIN	MURDER
SCHOOL	PRESIDENT	SUTTER	JOHNNY	POISON

FEAR	HOME	BRIDGE	ROCK	MARY
FIELD	MURDER	JOHNNY	SARA	COLLEGE
LEANORA	WAGON	FREE SPACE	LEWIS	JEWS
SCHOOL	KKK	HOLLOWEEN	GALOSHES	HIRSH
TRAIN	VIOLA	PERCELLE	PRESIDENT	NEWSPAPER

POISON	BABY	HATE	ESTHER	REYNARD
MERLIN	CANE	IRIS	VOTE	MARRIED
JERRY	BROOMS	FREE SPACE	CROSS	PETTIBONE
HARVEY	FITZGERALD	POOR	KELLER	HOTEL
IRA	FRANKS	BRANDED	HEAVEN	KIDNAPPING

COLLEGE	JOHNNY	VIOLA	IRIS	REYNARD
JERRY	FITZGERALD	SARA	TRAIN	PETTIBONE
PRESIDENT	ROCK	FREE SPACE	BROOMS	REEVES
FRANKS	PERCELLE	CANE	MARY	WAGON
LEANORA	HATE	BRIDGE	POOR	BABY

FIELD	HARVEY	ESTHER	SUTTER	NEWSPAPER
LEWIS	HOTEL	MURDER	JEWS	FEAR
GALOSHES	SCHOOL	FREE SPACE	KKK	CAR
BRANDED	POISON	KELLER	LEOPOLD	CROSS
HIRSH	HOME	MERLIN	HOLLOWEEN	IRA

HOLLOWEEN	JOHNNY	MARY	WAGON	REEVES
MURDER	LEOPOLD	JERRY	FRANKS	MERLIN
ESTHER	KELLER	FREE SPACE	ROCK	SUTTER
GALOSHES	REYNARD	POISON	PRESIDENT	TRAIN
FEAR	NEWSPAPER	IRA	LEANORA	VOTE

FITZGERALD	BRIDGE	HIRSH	COLLEGE	VIOLA
CAR	KKK	PERCELLE	HOTEL	HOME
HARVEY	FIELD	FREE SPACE	SARA	MARRIED
POOR	HATE	KIDNAPPING	JEWS	HEAVEN
IRIS	LEWIS	PETTIBONE	CANE	BROOMS

LEANORA	FIELD	VIOLA	FRANKS	BROOMS
CANE	JOHNNY	FITZGERALD	MARY	SCHOOL
PRESIDENT	SARA	FREE SPACE	FEAR	WAGON
HIRSH	MARRIED	HOME	HEAVEN	POOR
CROSS	SUTTER	MERLIN	COLLEGE	PETTIBONE

IRIS	BRIDGE	REYNARD	KKK	HATE
ROCK	LEWIS	TRAIN	BRANDED	PERCELLE
MURDER	KELLER	FREE SPACE	HOTEL	CAR
GALOSHES	ESTHER	POISON	REEVES	JERRY
NEWSPAPER	LEOPOLD	HOLLOWEEN	BABY	HARVEY

KELLER	PERCELLE	NEWSPAPER	PRESIDENT	ROCK
MURDER	CAR	SCHOOL	ESTHER	HARVEY
TRAIN	HOLLOWEEN	FREE SPACE	HEAVEN	JOHNNY
FITZGERALD	POOR	MARY	MERLIN	VIOLA
BROOMS	COLLEGE	HOME	REEVES	HIRSH

CROSS	WAGON	FEAR	BABY	GALOSHES
KIDNAPPING	SUTTER	HATE	LEOPOLD	KKK
LEANORA	FIELD	FREE SPACE	MARRIED	LEWIS
BRANDED	POISON	FRANKS	CANE	JERRY
SARA	IRA	IRIS	VOTE	HOTEL

CANE	SCHOOL	FIELD	CROSS	VOTE
BRIDGE	LEWIS	TRAIN	ESTHER	IRA
JOHNNY	FRANKS	FREE SPACE	WAGON	POOR
SARA	FEAR	PERCELLE	HOTEL	NEWSPAPER
MARRIED	CAR	LEOPOLD	FITZGERALD	BROOMS

VIOLA	PRESIDENT	KKK	HATE	BRANDED
REYNARD	JEWS	HOLLOWEEN	HEAVEN	REEVES
MURDER	ROCK	FREE SPACE	HIRSH	PETTIBONE
MERLIN	GALOSHES	SUTTER	HOME	KIDNAPPING
HARVEY	LEANORA	MARY	JERRY	IRIS

BRANDED	HOLLOWEEN	POISON	VOTE	ESTHER
BROOMS	ROCK	BABY	MURDER	CROSS
REEVES	PRESIDENT	FREE SPACE	HIRSH	FRANKS
JERRY	CANE	HARVEY	MARY	HOTEL
TRAIN	SUTTER	SCHOOL	FEAR	FITZGERALD

PETTIBONE	WAGON	FIELD	COLLEGE	HATE
VIOLA	SARA	KIDNAPPING	LEANORA	KKK
JEWS	IRA	FREE SPACE	PERCELLE	BRIDGE
KELLER	JOHNNY	MERLIN	LEWIS	GALOSHES
HEAVEN	CAR	POOR	NEWSPAPER	HOME

SARA	HOME	PRESIDENT	MARY	REYNARD
FRANKS	FITZGERALD	FIELD	IRIS	MERLIN
ROCK	TRAIN	FREE SPACE	CROSS	HEAVEN
BABY	BROOMS	CANE	LEWIS	HOLLOWEEN
LEANORA	JEWS	MURDER	WAGON	POISON

GALOSHES	KKK	HATE	POOR	VIOLA
MARRIED	COLLEGE	HARVEY	JOHNNY	SUTTER
JERRY	HOTEL	FREE SPACE	PETTIBONE	KIDNAPPING
ESTHER	PERCELLE	BRIDGE	LEOPOLD	FEAR
VOTE	HIRSH	REEVES	NEWSPAPER	BRANDED

WITNESS VOCABULARY WORD LIST

No.	Word	Clue/Definition
1.	ADVISING	Recommending; suggesting
2.	BRANDED	Symbol burned on with a hot iron
3.	BRIGADE	Large body of troops; a military unit
4.	CLERGYMAN	Christian minister
5.	CONDUCTED	The way a person acts, especially from the standpoint of morality and ethics
6.	CONSTABLE	Peace officer with less authority than a sheriff
7.	CRUCIFIX	A cross with the form of Jesus on it
8.	DECEPTIVE	Misleading; to make others believe something that is not true
9.	DESTITUTE	Lacking food, clothing, and shelter
10.	DICTATES	Guiding principles
11.	DIVINE	Supremely good or beautiful; magnificent
12.	ENDURE	Carry on despite hardships
13.	ENTWINED	Around or twisted together
14.	FIERCE	Furiously intense; wild; violent in force
15.	GALOSHES	Waterproof boot or shoe
16.	GANGLING	Awkwardly tall or long-limbed
17.	GRIEVES	Feels sorrow or distress
18.	GRUMBLE	Muttering a complaint
19.	IMPOSING	Very impressive because of great size, stately appearance, or dignity
20.	INCITING	Stirring up, encouraging or prompting into action
21.	INORDINATE	Exceeding reasonable limits; uncontrolled
22.	LUNATIC	Insane person
23.	LYNCHED	Hanged, as by a mob, without due process of the law
24.	MEEK	Tame; gentle; kind
25.	NEUTRAL	Belonging to neither side in a controversy
26.	PEERED	Looked intently, searchingly, or with difficulty
27.	PERDITION	Future state of the wicked; damnation; hell
28.	PERSECUTION	Punishment or harassment usually severe in nature based on race, religion, or political opinion
29.	PETITION	Formal request
30.	PINNACLE	The highest point, as with success, power, or fame
31.	RAIDING	Conducting a surprise attack on another's property with the purpose of taking goods
32.	RATTLED	Flustered; unnerved; confused
33.	REIGN	Rule or hold authority; dominate with power or influence
34.	RUBBISH	Nonsense; worthless material; garbage
35.	RUSTIC	Typical of country life of country people
36.	SANATORIUM	Institution for the treatment of certain chronic diseases or various nervous or mental disorders
37.	SCOLD	Reprimand or criticize harshly and usually angrily
38.	SENSIBLY	Showing good sense or sound judgment
39.	SPECTACLES	Eyeglasses
40.	STAMPEDE	Frenzied rush of a mass of people
41.	STOUT	Firm; strong; having endurance
42.	STRIFE	Conflict; struggle; clash
43.	STRUTTED	Walked in a pompous way
44.	UNSCRUPULOUS	Without principles
45.	URGING	Encouraging
46.	VEXED	Irritated; annoyed
47.	VIGILANT	On the alert; watchful

WITNESS VOCABULARY WORD LIST CONTINUED

No. Word	Clue/Definition
48. WIELD	Exercise power, or influence as in ruling or dominating
49. WRINGING	Extracting or expelling by twisting or compression

Witness Vocabulary Fill In The Blanks 1

1. Eyeglasses
2. Firm; strong; having endurance
3. On the alert; watchful
4. Insane person
5. Symbol burned on with a hot iron
6. The way a person acts, especially from the standpoint of morality and ethics
7. Typical of country life of country people
8. Walked in a pompous way
9. Stirring up, encouraging or prompting into action
10. Irritated; annoyed
11. Large body of troops; a military unit
12. Feels sorrow or distress
13. Very impressive because of great size, stately appearance, or dignity
14. Supremely good or beautiful; magnificent
15. Christian minister
16. Tame; gentle; kind
17. A cross with the form of Jesus on it
18. Conducting a surprise attack on another's property with the purpose of taking goods
19. Exceeding reasonable limits; uncontrolled
20. Future state of the wicked; damnation; hell

Witness Vocabulary Fill In The Blanks 1 Answer Key

SPECTACLES	1. Eyeglasses
STOUT	2. Firm; strong; having endurance
VIGILANT	3. On the alert; watchful
LUNATIC	4. Insane person
BRANDED	5. Symbol burned on with a hot iron
CONDUCTED	6. The way a person acts, especially from the standpoint of morality and ethics
RUSTIC	7. Typical of country life of country people
STRUTTED	8. Walked in a pompous way
INCITING	9. Stirring up, encouraging or prompting into action
VEXED	10. Irritated; annoyed
BRIGADE	11. Large body of troops; a military unit
GRIEVES	12. Feels sorrow or distress
IMPOSING	13. Very impressive because of great size, stately appearance, or dignity
DIVINE	14. Supremely good or beautiful; magnificent
CLERGYMAN	15. Christian minister
MEEK	16. Tame; gentle; kind
CRUCIFIX	17. A cross with the form of Jesus on it
RAIDING	18. Conducting a surprise attack on another's property with the purpose of taking goods
INORDINATE	19. Exceeding reasonable limits; uncontrolled
PERDITION	20. Future state of the wicked; damnation; hell

Witness Vocabulary Fill In The Blanks 2

1. Conflict; struggle; clash
2. Institution for the treatment of certain chronic diseases or various nervous or mental disorders
3. Exceeding reasonable limits; uncontrolled
4. Large body of troops; a military unit
5. Carry on despite hardships
6. Symbol burned on with a hot iron
7. Recommending; suggesting
8. Rule or hold authority; dominate with power or influence
9. Very impressive because of great size, stately appearance, or dignity
10. Awkwardly tall or long-limbed
11. Tame; gentle; kind
12. Peace officer with less authority than a sheriff
13. Insane person
14. The way a person acts, especially from the standpoint of morality and ethics
15. Typical of country life of country people
16. Lacking food, clothing, and shelter
17. Future state of the wicked; damnation; hell
18. Belonging to neither side in a controversy
19. Around or twisted together
20. Without principles

Witness Vocabulary Fill In The Blanks 2 Answer Key

STRIFE	1. Conflict; struggle; clash
SANATORIUM	2. Institution for the treatment of certain chronic diseases or various nervous or mental disorders
INORDINATE	3. Exceeding reasonable limits; uncontrolled
BRIGADE	4. Large body of troops; a military unit
ENDURE	5. Carry on despite hardships
BRANDED	6. Symbol burned on with a hot iron
ADVISING	7. Recommending; suggesting
REIGN	8. Rule or hold authority; dominate with power or influence
IMPOSING	9. Very impressive because of great size, stately appearance, or dignity
GANGLING	10. Awkwardly tall or long-limbed
MEEK	11. Tame; gentle; kind
CONSTABLE	12. Peace officer with less authority than a sheriff
LUNATIC	13. Insane person
CONDUCTED	14. The way a person acts, especially from the standpoint of morality and ethics
RUSTIC	15. Typical of country life of country people
DESTITUTE	16. Lacking food, clothing, and shelter
PERDITION	17. Future state of the wicked; damnation; hell
NEUTRAL	18. Belonging to neither side in a controversy
ENTWINED	19. Around or twisted together
UNSCRUPULOUS	20. Without principles

Witness Vocabulary Fill In The Blanks 3

1. On the alert; watchful
2. Large body of troops; a military unit
3. A cross with the form of Jesus on it
4. The highest point, as with success, power, or fame
5. Feels sorrow or distress
6. Conducting a surprise attack on another's property with the purpose of taking goods
7. Christian minister
8. Waterproof boot or shoe
9. Showing good sense or sound judgment
10. Typical of country life of country people
11. Guiding principles
12. Lacking food, clothing, and shelter
13. Irritated; annoyed
14. The way a person acts, especially from the standpoint of morality and ethics
15. Very impressive because of great size, stately appearance, or dignity
16. Frenzied rush of a mass of people
17. Exceeding reasonable limits; uncontrolled
18. Eyeglasses
19. Future state of the wicked; damnation; hell
20. Supremely good or beautiful; magnificent

Witness Vocabulary Fill In The Blanks 3 Answer Key

VIGILANT	1. On the alert; watchful
BRIGADE	2. Large body of troops; a military unit
CRUCIFIX	3. A cross with the form of Jesus on it
PINNACLE	4. The highest point, as with success, power, or fame
GRIEVES	5. Feels sorrow or distress
RAIDING	6. Conducting a surprise attack on another's property with the purpose of taking goods
CLERGYMAN	7. Christian minister
GALOSHES	8. Waterproof boot or shoe
SENSIBLY	9. Showing good sense or sound judgment
RUSTIC	10. Typical of country life of country people
DICTATES	11. Guiding principles
DESTITUTE	12. Lacking food, clothing, and shelter
VEXED	13. Irritated; annoyed
CONDUCTED	14. The way a person acts, especially from the standpoint of morality and ethics
IMPOSING	15. Very impressive because of great size, stately appearance, or dignity
STAMPEDE	16. Frenzied rush of a mass of people
INORDINATE	17. Exceeding reasonable limits; uncontrolled
SPECTACLES	18. Eyeglasses
PERDITION	19. Future state of the wicked; damnation; hell
DIVINE	20. Supremely good or beautiful; magnificent

Witness Vocabulary Fill In The Blanks 4

1. Tame; gentle; kind
2. Recommending; suggesting
3. Supremely good or beautiful; magnificent
4. Very impressive because of great size, stately appearance, or dignity
5. Punishment or harassment usually severe in nature based on race, religion, or political opinion
6. Insane person
7. Looked intently, searchingly, or with difficulty
8. Extracting or expelling by twisting or compression
9. Rule or hold authority; dominate with power or influence
10. Peace officer with less authority than a sheriff
11. Large body of troops; a military unit
12. Irritated; annoyed
13. Encouraging
14. On the alert; watchful
15. Eyeglasses
16. Flustered; unnerved; confused
17. Around or twisted together
18. Without principles
19. Misleading; to make others believe something that is not true
20. Hanged, as by a mob, without due process of the law

Witness Vocabulary Fill In The Blanks 4 Answer Key

MEEK	1. Tame; gentle; kind
ADVISING	2. Recommending; suggesting
DIVINE	3. Supremely good or beautiful; magnificent
IMPOSING	4. Very impressive because of great size, stately appearance, or dignity
PERSECUTION	5. Punishment or harassment usually severe in nature based on race, religion, or political opinion
LUNATIC	6. Insane person
PEERED	7. Looked intently, searchingly, or with difficulty
WRINGING	8. Extracting or expelling by twisting or compression
REIGN	9. Rule or hold authority; dominate with power or influence
CONSTABLE	10. Peace officer with less authority than a sheriff
BRIGADE	11. Large body of troops; a military unit
VEXED	12. Irritated; annoyed
URGING	13. Encouraging
VIGILANT	14. On the alert; watchful
SPECTACLES	15. Eyeglasses
RATTLED	16. Flustered; unnerved; confused
ENTWINED	17. Around or twisted together
UNSCRUPULOUS	18. Without principles
DECEPTIVE	19. Misleading; to make others believe something that is not true
LYNCHED	20. Hanged, as by a mob, without due process of the law

Witness Vocabulary Matching 1

___ 1. LUNATIC	A. Hanged, as by a mob, without due process of the law
___ 2. BRANDED	B. Reprimand or criticize harshly and usually angrily
___ 3. SENSIBLY	C. Conducting a surprise attack on another's property with the purpose of taking goods
___ 4. SCOLD	D. Showing good sense or sound judgment
___ 5. LYNCHED	E. Furiously intense; wild; violent in force
___ 6. IMPOSING	F. Waterproof boot or shoe
___ 7. SPECTACLES	G. Recommending; suggesting
___ 8. ADVISING	H. Encouraging
___ 9. WRINGING	I. Without principles
___10. STRIFE	J. Misleading; to make others believe something that is not true
___11. URGING	K. Punishment or harassment usually severe in nature based on race, religion, or political opinion
___12. PERSECUTION	L. Exercise power, or influence as in ruling or dominating
___13. GANGLING	M. Very impressive because of great size, stately appearance, or dignity
___14. RAIDING	N. Exceeding reasonable limits; uncontrolled
___15. ENDURE	O. Awkwardly tall or long-limbed
___16. WIELD	P. Irritated; annoyed
___17. DECEPTIVE	Q. Extracting or expelling by twisting or compression
___18. VEXED	R. Conflict; struggle; clash
___19. VIGILANT	S. Symbol burned on with a hot iron
___20. FIERCE	T. Future state of the wicked; damnation; hell
___21. GALOSHES	U. On the alert; watchful
___22. PERDITION	V. Eyeglasses
___23. UNSCRUPULOUS	W. Insane person
___24. NEUTRAL	X. Carry on despite hardships
___25. INORDINATE	Y. Belonging to neither side in a controversy

Witness Vocabulary Matching 1 Answer Key

W - 1. LUNATIC	A. Hanged, as by a mob, without due process of the law
S - 2. BRANDED	B. Reprimand or criticize harshly and usually angrily
D - 3. SENSIBLY	C. Conducting a surprise attack on another's property with the purpose of taking goods
B - 4. SCOLD	D. Showing good sense or sound judgment
A - 5. LYNCHED	E. Furiously intense; wild; violent in force
M - 6. IMPOSING	F. Waterproof boot or shoe
V - 7. SPECTACLES	G. Recommending; suggesting
G - 8. ADVISING	H. Encouraging
Q - 9. WRINGING	I. Without principles
R -10. STRIFE	J. Misleading; to make others believe something that is not true
H -11. URGING	K. Punishment or harassment usually severe in nature based on race, religion, or political opinion
K -12. PERSECUTION	L. Exercise power, or influence as in ruling or dominating
O -13. GANGLING	M. Very impressive because of great size, stately appearance, or dignity
C -14. RAIDING	N. Exceeding reasonable limits; uncontrolled
X -15. ENDURE	O. Awkwardly tall or long-limbed
L - 16. WIELD	P. Irritated; annoyed
J - 17. DECEPTIVE	Q. Extracting or expelling by twisting or compression
P -18. VEXED	R. Conflict; struggle; clash
U -19. VIGILANT	S. Symbol burned on with a hot iron
E -20. FIERCE	T. Future state of the wicked; damnation; hell
F -21. GALOSHES	U. On the alert; watchful
T -22. PERDITION	V. Eyeglasses
I - 23. UNSCRUPULOUS	W. Insane person
Y -24. NEUTRAL	X. Carry on despite hardships
N -25. INORDINATE	Y. Belonging to neither side in a controversy

Witness Vocabulary Matching 2

___ 1. REIGN	A. Looked intently, searchingly, or with difficulty
___ 2. CONDUCTED	B. Nonsense; worthless material; garbage
___ 3. UNSCRUPULOUS	C. Institution for the treatment of certain chronic diseases or various nervous or mental disorders
___ 4. ADVISING	D. Exercise power, or influence as in ruling or dominating
___ 5. WIELD	E. Punishment or harassment usually severe in nature based on race, religion, or political opinion
___ 6. CLERGYMAN	F. Supremely good or beautiful; magnificent
___ 7. MEEK	G. Insane person
___ 8. SANATORIUM	H. Tame; gentle; kind
___ 9. LYNCHED	I. Stirring up, encouraging or prompting into action
___10. ENTWINED	J. Christian minister
___11. LUNATIC	K. Without principles
___12. SCOLD	L. Future state of the wicked; damnation; hell
___13. DESTITUTE	M. The way a person acts, especially from the standpoint of morality and ethics
___14. DIVINE	N. Recommending; suggesting
___15. VEXED	O. A cross with the form of Jesus on it
___16. URGING	P. Encouraging
___17. CRUCIFIX	Q. Reprimand or criticize harshly and usually angrily
___18. PEERED	R. The highest point, as with success, power, or fame
___19. RUBBISH	S. Hanged, as by a mob, without due process of the law
___20. GRUMBLE	T. Around or twisted together
___21. SENSIBLY	U. Showing good sense or sound judgment
___22. PINNACLE	V. Irritated; annoyed
___23. PERSECUTION	W. Lacking food, clothing, and shelter
___24. PERDITION	X. Rule or hold authority; dominate with power or influence
___25. INCITING	Y. Muttering a complaint

Witness Vocabulary Matching 2 Answer Key

X - 1. REIGN	A. Looked intently, searchingly, or with difficulty
M - 2. CONDUCTED	B. Nonsense; worthless material; garbage
K - 3. UNSCRUPULOUS	C. Institution for the treatment of certain chronic diseases or various nervous or mental disorders
N - 4. ADVISING	D. Exercise power, or influence as in ruling or dominating
D - 5. WIELD	E. Punishment or harassment usually severe in nature based on race, religion, or political opinion
J - 6. CLERGYMAN	F. Supremely good or beautiful; magnificent
H - 7. MEEK	G. Insane person
C - 8. SANATORIUM	H. Tame; gentle; kind
S - 9. LYNCHED	I. Stirring up, encouraging or prompting into action
T -10. ENTWINED	J. Christian minister
G -11. LUNATIC	K. Without principles
Q -12. SCOLD	L. Future state of the wicked; damnation; hell
W -13. DESTITUTE	M. The way a person acts, especially from the standpoint of morality and ethics
F -14. DIVINE	N. Recommending; suggesting
V -15. VEXED	O. A cross with the form of Jesus on it
P -16. URGING	P. Encouraging
O -17. CRUCIFIX	Q. Reprimand or criticize harshly and usually angrily
A -18. PEERED	R. The highest point, as with success, power, or fame
B -19. RUBBISH	S. Hanged, as by a mob, without due process of the law
Y -20. GRUMBLE	T. Around or twisted together
U -21. SENSIBLY	U. Showing good sense or sound judgment
R -22. PINNACLE	V. Irritated; annoyed
E -23. PERSECUTION	W. Lacking food, clothing, and shelter
L -24. PERDITION	X. Rule or hold authority; dominate with power or influence
I - 25. INCITING	Y. Muttering a complaint

Witness Vocabulary Matching 3

___ 1. DESTITUTE	A. Very impressive because of great size, stately appearance, or dignity
___ 2. VIGILANT	B. Recommending; suggesting
___ 3. PINNACLE	C. Rule or hold authority; dominate with power or influence
___ 4. SENSIBLY	D. Punishment or harassment usually severe in nature based on race, religion, or political opinion
___ 5. LUNATIC	E. Feels sorrow or distress
___ 6. GALOSHES	F. Hanged, as by a mob, without due process of the law
___ 7. RAIDING	G. Irritated; annoyed
___ 8. BRIGADE	H. Peace officer with less authority than a sheriff
___ 9. GANGLING	I. Reprimand or criticize harshly and usually angrily
___10. DICTATES	J. Insane person
___11. BRANDED	K. Misleading; to make others believe something that is not true
___12. PERSECUTION	L. Guiding principles
___13. IMPOSING	M. Conflict; struggle; clash
___14. CONSTABLE	N. On the alert; watchful
___15. SCOLD	O. Waterproof boot or shoe
___16. NEUTRAL	P. Carry on despite hardships
___17. ADVISING	Q. Showing good sense or sound judgment
___18. REIGN	R. Lacking food, clothing, and shelter
___19. DECEPTIVE	S. Furiously intense; wild; violent in force
___20. FIERCE	T. Symbol burned on with a hot iron
___21. STRIFE	U. Large body of troops; a military unit
___22. LYNCHED	V. Conducting a surprise attack on another's property with the purpose of taking goods
___23. ENDURE	W. Belonging to neither side in a controversy
___24. VEXED	X. The highest point, as with success, power, or fame
___25. GRIEVES	Y. Awkwardly tall or long-limbed

Witness Vocabulary Matching 3 Answer Key

R - 1. DESTITUTE	A. Very impressive because of great size, stately appearance, or dignity
N - 2. VIGILANT	B. Recommending; suggesting
X - 3. PINNACLE	C. Rule or hold authority; dominate with power or influence
Q - 4. SENSIBLY	D. Punishment or harassment usually severe in nature based on race, religion, or political opinion
J - 5. LUNATIC	E. Feels sorrow or distress
O - 6. GALOSHES	F. Hanged, as by a mob, without due process of the law
V - 7. RAIDING	G. Irritated; annoyed
U - 8. BRIGADE	H. Peace officer with less authority than a sheriff
Y - 9. GANGLING	I. Reprimand or criticize harshly and usually angrily
L - 10. DICTATES	J. Insane person
T - 11. BRANDED	K. Misleading; to make others believe something that is not true
D - 12. PERSECUTION	L. Guiding principles
A - 13. IMPOSING	M. Conflict; struggle; clash
H - 14. CONSTABLE	N. On the alert; watchful
I - 15. SCOLD	O. Waterproof boot or shoe
W - 16. NEUTRAL	P. Carry on despite hardships
B - 17. ADVISING	Q. Showing good sense or sound judgment
C - 18. REIGN	R. Lacking food, clothing, and shelter
K - 19. DECEPTIVE	S. Furiously intense; wild; violent in force
S - 20. FIERCE	T. Symbol burned on with a hot iron
M - 21. STRIFE	U. Large body of troops; a military unit
F - 22. LYNCHED	V. Conducting a surprise attack on another's property with the purpose of taking goods
P - 23. ENDURE	W. Belonging to neither side in a controversy
G - 24. VEXED	X. The highest point, as with success, power, or fame
E - 25. GRIEVES	Y. Awkwardly tall or long-limbed

Witness Vocabulary Matching 4

___ 1. NEUTRAL	A. Encouraging
___ 2. ADVISING	B. Lacking food, clothing, and shelter
___ 3. PERSECUTION	C. Guiding principles
___ 4. BRIGADE	D. Conducting a surprise attack on another's property with the purpose of taking goods
___ 5. GRUMBLE	E. Flustered; unnerved; confused
___ 6. RAIDING	F. Belonging to neither side in a controversy
___ 7. RATTLED	G. Muttering a complaint
___ 8. INCITING	H. Institution for the treatment of certain chronic diseases or various nervous or mental disorders
___ 9. BRANDED	I. Misleading; to make others believe something that is not true
___10. DICTATES	J. Tame; gentle; kind
___11. CONSTABLE	K. Furiously intense; wild; violent in force
___12. LYNCHED	L. Symbol burned on with a hot iron
___13. DESTITUTE	M. Formal request
___14. URGING	N. Hanged, as by a mob, without due process of the law
___15. PETITION	O. Punishment or harassment usually severe in nature based on race, religion, or political opinion
___16. GALOSHES	P. Christian minister
___17. VEXED	Q. Extracting or expelling by twisting or compression
___18. ENTWINED	R. Waterproof boot or shoe
___19. DIVINE	S. Around or twisted together
___20. FIERCE	T. Large body of troops; a military unit
___21. DECEPTIVE	U. Irritated; annoyed
___22. WRINGING	V. Supremely good or beautiful; magnificent
___23. MEEK	W. Peace officer with less authority than a sheriff
___24. SANATORIUM	X. Stirring up, encouraging or prompting into action
___25. CLERGYMAN	Y. Recommending; suggesting

Witness Vocabulary Matching 4 Answer Key

F - 1. NEUTRAL	A. Encouraging
Y - 2. ADVISING	B. Lacking food, clothing, and shelter
O - 3. PERSECUTION	C. Guiding principles
T - 4. BRIGADE	D. Conducting a surprise attack on another's property with the purpose of taking goods
G - 5. GRUMBLE	E. Flustered; unnerved; confused
D - 6. RAIDING	F. Belonging to neither side in a controversy
E - 7. RATTLED	G. Muttering a complaint
X - 8. INCITING	H. Institution for the treatment of certain chronic diseases or various nervous or mental disorders
L - 9. BRANDED	I. Misleading; to make others believe something that is not true
C -10. DICTATES	J. Tame; gentle; kind
W -11. CONSTABLE	K. Furiously intense; wild; violent in force
N -12. LYNCHED	L. Symbol burned on with a hot iron
B -13. DESTITUTE	M. Formal request
A -14. URGING	N. Hanged, as by a mob, without due process of the law
M -15. PETITION	O. Punishment or harassment usually severe in nature based on race, religion, or political opinion
R -16. GALOSHES	P. Christian minister
U -17. VEXED	Q. Extracting or expelling by twisting or compression
S -18. ENTWINED	R. Waterproof boot or shoe
V -19. DIVINE	S. Around or twisted together
K -20. FIERCE	T. Large body of troops; a military unit
I - 21. DECEPTIVE	U. Irritated; annoyed
Q -22. WRINGING	V. Supremely good or beautiful; magnificent
J - 23. MEEK	W. Peace officer with less authority than a sheriff
H -24. SANATORIUM	X. Stirring up, encouraging or prompting into action
P -25. CLERGYMAN	Y. Recommending; suggesting

Witness Vocabulary Magic Squares 1

A. PERDITION
B. IMPOSING
C. RUSTIC
D. URGING
E. RATTLED
F. STAMPEDE
G. SANATORIUM
H. CONSTABLE
I. VIGILANT
J. GRUMBLE
K. BRANDED
L. LYNCHED
M. UNSCRUPULOUS
N. FIERCE
O. STRIFE
P. CLERGYMAN

1. Peace officer with less authority than a sheriff
2. Future state of the wicked; damnation; hell
3. Very impressive because of great size, stately appearance, or dignity
4. Institution for the treatment of certain chronic diseases or various nervous or mental disorders
5. Muttering a complaint
6. Conflict; struggle; clash
7. Christian minister
8. On the alert; watchful
9. Symbol burned on with a hot iron
10. Furiously intense; wild; violent in force
11. Without principles
12. Hanged, as by a mob, without due process of the law
13. Flustered; unnerved; confused
14. Encouraging
15. Typical of country life of country people
16. Frenzied rush of a mass of people

A=	B=	C=	D=
E=	F=	G=	H=
I=	J=	K=	L=
M=	N=	O=	P=

Witness Vocabulary Magic Squares 1 Answer Key

A. PERDITION
B. IMPOSING
C. RUSTIC
D. URGING
E. RATTLED
F. STAMPEDE
G. SANATORIUM
H. CONSTABLE
I. VIGILANT
J. GRUMBLE
K. BRANDED
L. LYNCHED
M. UNSCRUPULOUS
N. FIERCE
O. STRIFE
P. CLERGYMAN

1. Peace officer with less authority than a sheriff
2. Future state of the wicked; damnation; hell
3. Very impressive because of great size, stately appearance, or dignity
4. Institution for the treatment of certain chronic diseases or various nervous or mental disorders
5. Muttering a complaint
6. Conflict; struggle; clash
7. Christian minister
8. On the alert; watchful
9. Symbol burned on with a hot iron
10. Furiously intense; wild; violent in force
11. Without principles
12. Hanged, as by a mob, without due process of the law
13. Flustered; unnerved; confused
14. Encouraging
15. Typical of country life of country people
16. Frenzied rush of a mass of people

A=2	B=3	C=15	D=14
E=13	F=16	G=4	H=1
I=8	J=5	K=9	L=12
M=11	N=10	O=6	P=7

Witness Vocabulary Magic Squares 2

A. DECEPTIVE
B. BRANDED
C. WIELD
D. STAMPEDE
E. STOUT
F. INORDINATE
G. RATTLED
H. SCOLD
I. DICTATES
J. VIGILANT
K. MEEK
L. PEERED
M. STRUTTED
N. DIVINE
O. ADVISING
P. CLERGYMAN

1. Misleading; to make others believe something that is not true
2. Supremely good or beautiful; magnificent
3. On the alert; watchful
4. Firm; strong; having endurance
5. Flustered; unnerved; confused
6. Looked intently, searchingly, or with difficulty
7. Christian minister
8. Exercise power, or influence as in ruling or dominating
9. Recommending; suggesting
10. Frenzied rush of a mass of people
11. Reprimand or criticize harshly and usually angrily
12. Tame; gentle; kind
13. Guiding principles
14. Exceeding reasonable limits; uncontrolled
15. Symbol burned on with a hot iron
16. Walked in a pompous way

A=	B=	C=	D=
E=	F=	G=	H=
I=	J=	K=	L=
M=	N=	O=	P=

Witness Vocabulary Magic Squares 2 Answer Key

A. DECEPTIVE
B. BRANDED
C. WIELD
D. STAMPEDE
E. STOUT
F. INORDINATE
G. RATTLED
H. SCOLD
I. DICTATES
J. VIGILANT
K. MEEK
L. PEERED
M. STRUTTED
N. DIVINE
O. ADVISING
P. CLERGYMAN

1. Misleading; to make others believe something that is not true
2. Supremely good or beautiful; magnificent
3. On the alert; watchful
4. Firm; strong; having endurance
5. Flustered; unnerved; confused
6. Looked intently, searchingly, or with difficulty
7. Christian minister
8. Exercise power, or influence as in ruling or dominating
9. Recommending; suggesting
10. Frenzied rush of a mass of people
11. Reprimand or criticize harshly and usually angrily
12. Tame; gentle; kind
13. Guiding principles
14. Exceeding reasonable limits; uncontrolled
15. Symbol burned on with a hot iron
16. Walked in a pompous way

A=1	B=15	C=8	D=10
E=4	F=14	G=5	H=11
I=13	J=3	K=12	L=6
M=16	N=2	O=9	P=7

Witness Vocabulary Magic Squares 3

A. RUBBISH	E. SANATORIUM	I. IMPOSING	M. STRUTTED
B. STAMPEDE	F. INCITING	J. LUNATIC	N. BRANDED
C. DECEPTIVE	G. CLERGYMAN	K. UNSCRUPULOUS	O. GALOSHES
D. ADVISING	H. FIERCE	L. LYNCHED	P. GRIEVES

1. Waterproof boot or shoe
2. Insane person
3. Furiously intense; wild; violent in force
4. Nonsense; worthless material; garbage
5. Recommending; suggesting
6. Institution for the treatment of certain chronic diseases or various nervous or mental disorders
7. Without principles
8. Symbol burned on with a hot iron
9. Stirring up, encouraging or prompting into action
10. Misleading; to make others believe something that is not true
11. Walked in a pompous way
12. Hanged, as by a mob, without due process of the law
13. Very impressive because of great size, stately appearance, or dignity
14. Feels sorrow or distress
15. Frenzied rush of a mass of people
16. Christian minister

A=	B=	C=	D=
E=	F=	G=	H=
I=	J=	K=	L=
M=	N=	O=	P=

Witness Vocabulary Magic Squares 3 Answer Key

A. RUBBISH
B. STAMPEDE
C. DECEPTIVE
D. ADVISING
E. SANATORIUM
F. INCITING
G. CLERGYMAN
H. FIERCE
I. IMPOSING
J. LUNATIC
K. UNSCRUPULOUS
L. LYNCHED
M. STRUTTED
N. BRANDED
O. GALOSHES
P. GRIEVES

1. Waterproof boot or shoe
2. Insane person
3. Furiously intense; wild; violent in force
4. Nonsense; worthless material; garbage
5. Recommending; suggesting
6. Institution for the treatment of certain chronic diseases or various nervous or mental disorders
7. Without principles
8. Symbol burned on with a hot iron
9. Stirring up, encouraging or prompting into action
10. Misleading; to make others believe something that is not true
11. Walked in a pompous way
12. Hanged, as by a mob, without due process of the law
13. Very impressive because of great size, stately appearance, or dignity
14. Feels sorrow or distress
15. Frenzied rush of a mass of people
16. Christian minister

A=4	B=15	C=10	D=5
E=6	F=9	G=16	H=3
I=13	J=2	K=7	L=12
M=11	N=8	O=1	P=14

Witness Vocabulary Magic Squares 4

A. CONDUCTED
B. LUNATIC
C. ENTWINED
D. DESTITUTE
E. RUBBISH
F. SPECTACLES
G. PERSECUTION
H. UNSCRUPULOUS
I. FIERCE
J. STRIFE
K. RUSTIC
L. URGING
M. GRIEVES
N. ADVISING
O. PINNACLE
P. GANGLING

1. The highest point, as with success, power, or fame
2. Lacking food, clothing, and shelter
3. Conflict; struggle; clash
4. Nonsense; worthless material; garbage
5. Furiously intense; wild; violent in force
6. Eyeglasses
7. Awkwardly tall or long-limbed
8. Around or twisted together
9. Without principles
10. Typical of country life of country people
11. The way a person acts, especially from the standpoint of morality and ethics
12. Recommending; suggesting
13. Insane person
14. Feels sorrow or distress
15. Punishment or harassment usually severe in nature based on race, religion, or political opinion
16. Encouraging

A=	B=	C=	D=
E=	F=	G=	H=
I=	J=	K=	L=
M=	N=	O=	P=

Witness Vocabulary Magic Squares 4 Answer Key

A. CONDUCTED
B. LUNATIC
C. ENTWINED
D. DESTITUTE
E. RUBBISH
F. SPECTACLES
G. PERSECUTION
H. UNSCRUPULOUS
I. FIERCE
J. STRIFE
K. RUSTIC
L. URGING
M. GRIEVES
N. ADVISING
O. PINNACLE
P. GANGLING

1. The highest point, as with success, power, or fame
2. Lacking food, clothing, and shelter
3. Conflict; struggle; clash
4. Nonsense; worthless material; garbage
5. Furiously intense; wild; violent in force
6. Eyeglasses
7. Awkwardly tall or long-limbed
8. Around or twisted together
9. Without principles
10. Typical of country life of country people
11. The way a person acts, especially from the standpoint of morality and ethics
12. Recommending; suggesting
13. Insane person
14. Feels sorrow or distress
15. Punishment or harassment usually severe in nature based on race, religion, or political opinion
16. Encouraging

A=11	B=13	C=8	D=2
E=4	F=6	G=15	H=9
I=5	J=3	K=10	L=16
M=14	N=12	O=1	P=7

Witness Vocabulary Word Search 1

F	I	E	R	C	E	Z	E	G	D	I	V	I	N	E	V	W	D	K	Q
D	C	F	N	O	S	A	N	A	T	O	R	I	U	M	I	H	E	B	R
G	R	J	L	N	W	S	D	N	C	Y	L	C	W	R	G	J	S	N	T
B	U	X	J	S	Q	L	U	G	D	J	T	V	Y	W	I	V	T	J	P
W	C	G	G	T	B	B	R	L	P	L	G	R	C	R	L	E	I	D	X
Q	I	B	X	A	D	R	E	I	L	R	D	W	U	W	A	X	T	S	C
M	F	R	C	B	E	I	I	N	W	P	H	R	I	S	N	E	U	E	F
C	I	A	W	L	C	N	P	G	R	U	M	B	L	E	T	D	T	N	Y
O	X	N	R	E	E	O	T	E	A	A	W	F	P	J	L	I	E	S	K
N	P	D	I	C	P	R	B	W	E	D	I	D	E	M	D	D	C	I	L
D	J	E	N	H	T	D	G	C	I	R	E	D	T	K	X	N	D	B	G
U	Y	D	G	F	I	I	R	Y	W	N	E	P	I	N	N	A	C	L	E
C	T	T	I	B	V	N	M	U	M	T	E	D	T	N	F	G	I	Y	Y
T	H	K	N	B	E	A	N	P	B	A	Y	D	I	L	G	R	N	U	D
E	W	H	G	B	D	T	E	M	O	B	N	C	O	Y	Y	I	C	R	S
D	S	T	R	I	F	E	U	E	S	S	I	Q	N	N	R	E	I	G	N
R	A	T	T	L	E	D	T	E	T	F	I	S	P	C	L	V	T	I	Q
L	J	L	W	P	S	B	R	K	O	F	P	N	H	H	Z	E	I	N	Q
L	U	N	A	T	I	C	A	V	U	H	L	V	G	E	W	S	N	G	C
S	C	O	L	D	Y	S	L	S	T	A	M	P	E	D	E	T	G	Q	J

Flustered; unnerved; confused (7)
Looked intently, searchingly, or with difficulty (6)
A cross with the form of Jesus on it (8)
Around or twisted together (8)
Awkwardly tall or long-limbed (8)
Belonging to neither side in a controversy (7)
Carry on despite hardships (6)
Christian minister (9)
Conducting a surprise attack on another's property with the purpose of taking goods (7)
Conflict; struggle; clash (6)
Encouraging (6)
Exceeding reasonable limits; uncontrolled (10)
Exercise power, or influence as in ruling or dominating (5)
Extracting or expelling by twisting or compression (8)
Feels sorrow or distress (7)
Firm; strong; having endurance (5)
Formal request (8)
Frenzied rush of a mass of people (8)
Furiously intense; wild; violent in force (6)
Hanged, as by a mob, without due process of the law (7)
Insane person (7)
Institution for the treatment of certain chronic diseases or various nervous or mental disorders (10

Irritated; annoyed (5)
Lacking food, clothing, and shelter (9)
Large body of troops; a military unit (7)
Misleading; to make others believe something that is not true (9)
Muttering a complaint (7)
Nonsense; worthless material; garbage (7)
On the alert; watchful (8)
Peace officer with less authority than a sheriff (9)
Reprimand or criticize harshly and usually angrily (5)
Rule or hold authority; dominate with power or influence (5)
Showing good sense or sound judgment (8)
Stirring up, encouraging or prompting into action (8)
Supremely good or beautiful; magnificent (6)
Symbol burned on with a hot iron (7)
Tame; gentle; kind (4)
The highest point, as with success, power, or fame (8)
The way a person acts, especially from the standpoint of morality and ethics (9)
Typical of country life of country people (6)
Very impressive because of great size, stately appearance, or dignity (8)

Witness Vocabulary Word Search 1 Answer Key

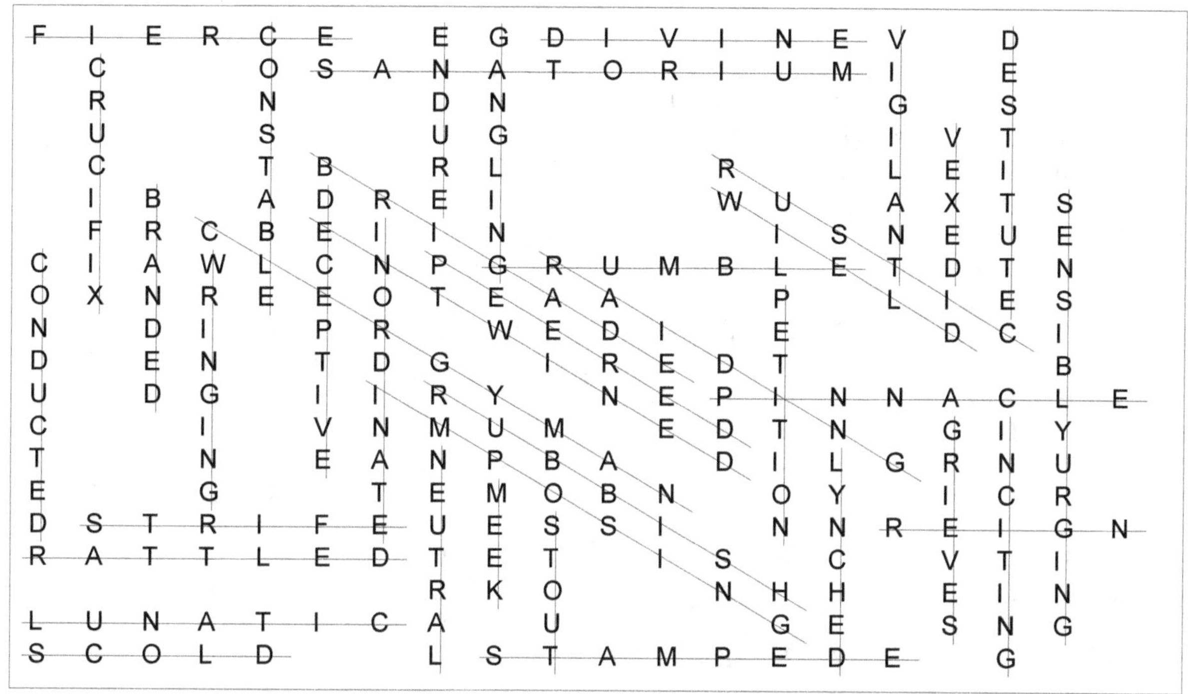

Flustered; unnerved; confused (7)
Looked intently, searchingly, or with difficulty (6)
A cross with the form of Jesus on it (8)
Around or twisted together (8)
Awkwardly tall or long-limbed (8)
Belonging to neither side in a controversy (7)
Carry on despite hardships (6)
Christian minister (9)
Conducting a surprise attack on another's property with the purpose of taking goods (7)
Conflict; struggle; clash (6)
Encouraging (6)
Exceeding reasonable limits; uncontrolled (10)
Exercise power, or influence as in ruling or dominating (5)
Extracting or expelling by twisting or compression (8)
Feels sorrow or distress (7)
Firm; strong; having endurance (5)
Formal request (8)
Frenzied rush of a mass of people (8)
Furiously intense; wild; violent in force (6)
Hanged, as by a mob, without due process of the law (7)
Insane person (7)
Institution for the treatment of certain chronic diseases or various nervous or mental disorders (10

Irritated; annoyed (5)
Lacking food, clothing, and shelter (9)
Large body of troops; a military unit (7)
Misleading; to make others believe something that is not true (9)
Muttering a complaint (7)
Nonsense; worthless material; garbage (7)
On the alert; watchful (8)
Peace officer with less authority than a sheriff (9)
Reprimand or criticize harshly and usually angrily (5)
Rule or hold authority; dominate with power or influence (5)
Showing good sense or sound judgment (8)
Stirring up, encouraging or prompting into action (8)
Supremely good or beautiful; magnificent (6)
Symbol burned on with a hot iron (7)
Tame; gentle; kind (4)
The highest point, as with success, power, or fame (8)
The way a person acts, especially from the standpoint of morality and ethics (9)
Typical of country life of country people (6)
Very impressive because of great size, stately appearance, or dignity (8)

Witness Vocabulary Word Search 2

P	E	R	D	I	T	I	O	N	C	Z	C	P	R	S	T	O	U	T	J
D	S	S	I	M	N	U	R	G	I	N	G	R	I	A	C	M	E	E	K
E	E	T	N	P	G	C	F	W	H	F	K	N	U	N	T	O	J	G	W
S	N	A	O	O	A	A	I	S	T	R	I	F	E	C	N	T	L	H	Q
T	S	M	R	S	L	D	N	T	P	B	Q	R	G	U	I	A	L	D	P
I	I	P	D	I	O	P	V	G	I	M	R	T	C	R	T	F	C	E	J
T	B	E	I	N	S	E	I	I	L	N	G	A	O	G	U	R	I	L	D
U	L	D	N	G	H	T	G	J	S	I	G	H	N	N	V	M	A	X	E
T	Y	E	A	M	E	I	I	V	X	I	N	C	S	D	K	T	B	L	L
E	S	C	T	Z	S	T	L	F	P	W	N	G	T	D	E	D	G	L	J
R	T	L	E	Y	J	I	A	V	E	I	S	G	A	B	M	D	R	P	E
U	R	E	S	M	S	O	N	X	R	E	G	G	B	D	X	R	I	B	W
B	U	R	D	T	G	N	T	F	S	L	D	F	L	C	V	E	E	P	T
B	T	G	B	L	Y	N	C	H	E	D	E	C	E	P	T	I	V	E	W
I	T	Y	R	R	X	Y	F	M	C	Q	I	N	K	V	B	G	E	E	X
S	E	M	I	U	F	T	I	R	U	B	D	V	D	D	E	N	S	R	X
H	D	A	G	S	Q	Z	E	G	T	P	L	H	I	U	M	X	K	E	J
L	U	N	A	T	I	C	R	A	I	D	I	N	G	N	R	B	E	D	V
Z	V	T	D	I	X	D	C	W	O	P	S	N	G	R	E	E	H	D	S
Y	M	L	E	C	X	Y	E	Z	N	S	A	N	A	T	O	R	I	U	M

Flustered; unnerved; confused (7)
Looked intently, searchingly, or with difficulty (6)
A cross with the form of Jesus on it (8)
Awkwardly tall or long-limbed (8)
Belonging to neither side in a controversy (7)
Carry on despite hardships (6)
Christian minister (9)
Conducting a surprise attack on another's property with the purpose of taking goods (7)
Conflict; struggle; clash (6)
Encouraging (6)
Exceeding reasonable limits; uncontrolled (10)
Exercise power, or influence as in ruling or dominating (5)
Feels sorrow or distress (7)
Firm; strong; having endurance (5)
Formal request (8)
Frenzied rush of a mass of people (8)
Furiously intense; wild; violent in force (6)
Future state of the wicked; damnation; hell (9)
Hanged, as by a mob, without due process of the law (7)
Insane person (7)
Institution for the treatment of certain chronic diseases or various nervous or mental disorders (10
Irritated; annoyed (5)
Lacking food, clothing, and shelter (9)
Large body of troops; a military unit (7)
Misleading; to make others believe something that is not true (9)
Muttering a complaint (7)
Nonsense; worthless material; garbage (7)
On the alert; watchful (8)
Peace officer with less authority than a sheriff (9)
Punishment or harassment usually severe in nature based on race, religion, or political opinion (11)
Recommending; suggesting (8)
Reprimand or criticize harshly and usually angrily (5)
Rule or hold authority; dominate with power or influence (5)
Showing good sense or sound judgment (8)
Stirring up, encouraging or prompting into action (8)
Supremely good or beautiful; magnificent (6)
Symbol burned on with a hot iron (7)
Tame; gentle; kind (4)
The highest point, as with success, power, or fame (8)
Typical of country life of country people (6)
Very impressive because of great size, stately appearance, or dignity (8)
Walked in a pompous way (8)
Waterproof boot or shoe (8)

Witness Vocabulary Word Search 2 Answer Key

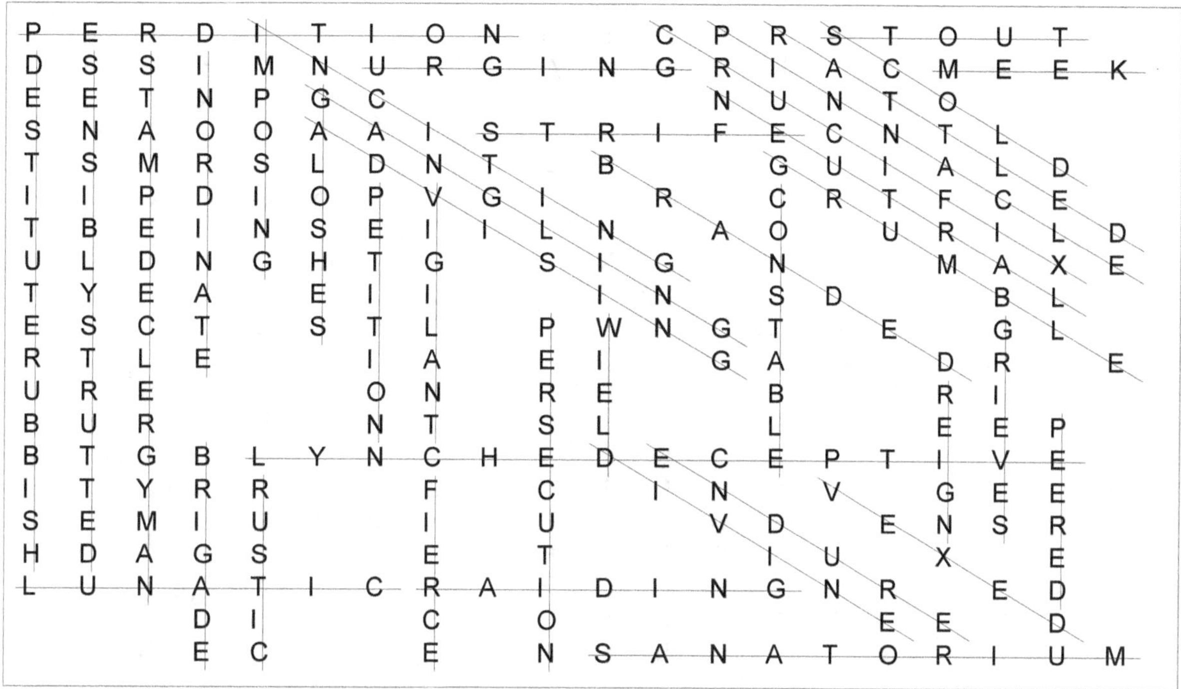

Flustered; unnerved; confused (7)
Looked intently, searchingly, or with difficulty (6)
A cross with the form of Jesus on it (8)
Awkwardly tall or long-limbed (8)
Belonging to neither side in a controversy (7)
Carry on despite hardships (6)
Christian minister (9)
Conducting a surprise attack on another's property with the purpose of taking goods (7)
Conflict; struggle; clash (6)
Encouraging (6)
Exceeding reasonable limits; uncontrolled (10)
Exercise power, or influence as in ruling or dominating (5)
Feels sorrow or distress (7)
Firm; strong; having endurance (5)
Formal request (8)
Frenzied rush of a mass of people (8)
Furiously intense; wild; violent in force (6)
Future state of the wicked; damnation; hell (9)
Hanged, as by a mob, without due process of the law (7)
Insane person (7)
Institution for the treatment of certain chronic diseases or various nervous or mental disorders (10
Irritated; annoyed (5)
Lacking food, clothing, and shelter (9)
Large body of troops; a military unit (7)
Misleading; to make others believe something that is not true (9)
Muttering a complaint (7)
Nonsense; worthless material; garbage (7)
On the alert; watchful (8)
Peace officer with less authority than a sheriff (9)
Punishment or harassment usually severe in nature based on race, religion, or political opinion (11)
Recommending; suggesting (8)
Reprimand or criticize harshly and usually angrily (5)
Rule or hold authority; dominate with power or influence (5)
Showing good sense or sound judgment (8)
Stirring up, encouraging or prompting into action (8)
Supremely good or beautiful; magnificent (6)
Symbol burned on with a hot iron (7)
Tame; gentle; kind (4)
The highest point, as with success, power, or fame (8)
Typical of country life of country people (6)
Very impressive because of great size, stately appearance, or dignity (8)
Walked in a pompous way (8)
Waterproof boot or shoe (8)

Witness Vocabulary Word Search 3

S B D L F H H M M B B G Z L B R V S W V
T F E W Y X T K C R A A U F R U I E L S
R N S R P N Y G K A D N R D I B G N X H
I S T I I S C W X N V G G J G B I S M K
F B I N N P C H R D I L I T A I L I E K
E R T G N E C P E E S I N S D S A B E L
F Y U I A C R A I D I N G T E H N L K L
C T T N C T U A J P N G C R C B T Y S V
G I E G L A C E T E G B N U I N S V C N
C R M Z E C I N P T A W D T S E Q E O L
L O U P N L F D E I L I P T T U V X L Y
E U N M O E I U E T O E M E A T I E D J
R K N S B S X R R I S L D D M R N D S H
G U M A T L I E E O H D Q B P A C I D H
Y D S M T A E N D N E Y D S E L I C L J
M Y I T H I B F G B S L T X D Z T T P J
A W S V I J C L F I E R C E E Z I A B C
N Q Y N I C D D E C E P T I V E N T P T
S T O U T N C O N D U C T E D T G E V B
E N T W I N E D P E R D I T I O N S S G

ADVISING	DICTATES	IMPOSING	PINNACLE	STAMPEDE
BRANDED	DIVINE	INCITING	RAIDING	STOUT
BRIGADE	ENDURE	LUNATIC	RATTLED	STRIFE
CLERGYMAN	ENTWINED	LYNCHED	REIGN	STRUTTED
CONDUCTED	FIERCE	MEEK	RUBBISH	URGING
CONSTABLE	GALOSHES	NEUTRAL	RUSTIC	VEXED
CRUCIFIX	GANGLING	PEERED	SCOLD	VIGILANT
DECEPTIVE	GRIEVES	PERDITION	SENSIBLY	WIELD
DESTITUTE	GRUMBLE	PETITION	SPECTACLES	WRINGING

Witness Vocabulary Word Search 3 Answer Key

S		D	L						B		G			B	R	V	S	
T		E	W	Y					R	A	A	U		R	U	I	E	
R		S	R	P	N				A	D	N	R		I	B	G	N	
I		T	I	I	S	C			N	V	G	G		G	B	I	S	M
F		I	N	N	P		H	R	D	I	L	I		A	I	L	I	E
E		T	G	N	E	C		E	E	S	I	N	S	D	S	A	B	E
		U	I	A	C	R	A	I	D	I	N	G	T	E	H	N	L	K
		T	N	C	T	U	A		P	N	G		R			T	Y	S
G	I	E	G	L	A	C	E	T	E	G		N	U	I	N		V	C
C	R	M		E	C	I	N	P	T	A	W		T	S	E		E	O
L	O	U	P		L	F	D	E	I	L	I		T	T	U	V	X	L
E	U	N	M	O	E	I	U	E	T	O	E		E	A	T	I	E	D
R		N	S	B	S	X	R	R	I	S	L	D	D	M	R	N	D	S
G	U		A	T	L	I	E	E	O	H	D			P	A	C	I	
Y	D	S		T	A	E	N	D	N	E				E	L	I	C	
M		I	T		I	B		G		S				D		T	T	
A			V	I		C	L	F	I	E	R	C	E	E		I	A	
N				I	C		D	E	C	E	P	T	I	V	E	N	T	
S	T	O	U	T	N	C	O	N	D	U	C	T	E	D		G	E	
E	N	T	W	I	N	E	D	P	E	R	D	I	T	I	O	N	S	

ADVISING	DICTATES	IMPOSING	PINNACLE	STAMPEDE
BRANDED	DIVINE	INCITING	RAIDING	STOUT
BRIGADE	ENDURE	LUNATIC	RATTLED	STRIFE
CLERGYMAN	ENTWINED	LYNCHED	REIGN	STRUTTED
CONDUCTED	FIERCE	MEEK	RUBBISH	URGING
CONSTABLE	GALOSHES	NEUTRAL	RUSTIC	VEXED
CRUCIFIX	GANGLING	PEERED	SCOLD	VIGILANT
DECEPTIVE	GRIEVES	PERDITION	SENSIBLY	WIELD
DESTITUTE	GRUMBLE	PETITION	SPECTACLES	WRINGING

Witness Vocabulary Word Search 4

R S E P U V S S R U B B I S H G W M F C
A P N E N R I E A U H R C R C V I E I P
I E T R S B G G N N S P A R D O E E E S
D C W S C R J I I S A T E N U G L K R M
I T I E R I P D N L I T I E D C D D C K
N A N C U G H C Q G A B O C R E I F E M
G C E U P A P O P Y F N L R K E D F D X
I L D T U D E N D U R E T Y I M D G I R
N E C I L E M D E H Y K L C M U T R C X
O S O O O C Y U S U M L C P P F M I T Y
R T N N U E V C T I T R R Q O Q K E A D
D A S A S P E T I S N R L E S P J V T F
I M T D G T X E T T T C A Y I T F E E D
N P A V R I E D U S J R I L N G R S S P
A E B I U V D W T S T O U T G C N I L X
T D L S M E I N E L U N A T I C H B F P
E E E I B B V R A T T L E D T N N E C E
X L W N L L I W R I N G I N G E G K D Q
F G R G E L N P I N N A C L E J D M Z B
Z T F C T P E R D I T I O N V G C T S H

ADVISING	DIVINE	LUNATIC	RATTLED	STOUT
BRANDED	ENDURE	LYNCHED	REIGN	STRIFE
BRIGADE	ENTWINED	MEEK	RUBBISH	STRUTTED
CONDUCTED	FIERCE	NEUTRAL	RUSTIC	UNSCRUPULOUS
CONSTABLE	GRIEVES	PEERED	SANATORIUM	URGING
CRUCIFIX	GRUMBLE	PERDITION	SCOLD	VEXED
DECEPTIVE	IMPOSING	PERSECUTION	SENSIBLY	VIGILANT
DESTITUTE	INCITING	PINNACLE	SPECTACLES	WIELD
DICTATES	INORDINATE	RAIDING	STAMPEDE	WRINGING

Witness Vocabulary Word Search 4 Answer Key

R	S	E	P	U	V	S	S	R	U	B	B	I	S	H		W	M	F	
A	P	N	E	N	R	I	E	A	U		R	C		C		I	E	I	
I	E	T	R	S	B	G	G	N	N	S	P	A	R		O	E	E	E	
D	C	W	S	C	R		I	I	S	A	T	E	N	U		L	K	R	
I	T	I	E	R	I			N	L	I	T	I	E	D	C	D	D	C	
N	A	N	C	U	G		C		G	A	B	O	C	R	E	I		E	
G	C	E	U	P	A		O				N	L	R		E	D	F	D	
I	L	D	T	U	D	E	N	D	U	R	E	T	Y	I		D	G	I	
N	E	C	I	L	E		D	E						M	U		R	C	X
O	S	O	O	O	C		U	S	U					P		M	I	T	
R	T	N	N	U	E	V	C	T	I	T		R		O			E	A	
D	A	S	A	S	P	E	T	I	S	N	R	L	E	S			V	T	
I	M	T	D	G	T	X	E	T		T	C	A	Y	I	T		E	E	
N	P	A	V	R	I	E	D	U			R	I	L	N	G	R	S	S	
A	E	B	I	U	V	D		T	S	T	O	U	T	G	C	N	I		
T	D	L	S	M	E	I		E	L	U	N	A	T	I	C	H		F	
E	E	E	I	B		V	R	A	T	T	L	E	D	T	N		E		E
			N	L		I	W	R	I	N	G	I	N	G	E	G		D	
			G	E		N	P	I	N	N	A	C	L	E		D			
					P	E	R	D	I	T	I	O	N						

ADVISING	DIVINE	LUNATIC	RATTLED	STOUT
BRANDED	ENDURE	LYNCHED	REIGN	STRIFE
BRIGADE	ENTWINED	MEEK	RUBBISH	STRUTTED
CONDUCTED	FIERCE	NEUTRAL	RUSTIC	UNSCRUPULOUS
CONSTABLE	GRIEVES	PEERED	SANATORIUM	URGING
CRUCIFIX	GRUMBLE	PERDITION	SCOLD	VEXED
DECEPTIVE	IMPOSING	PERSECUTION	SENSIBLY	VIGILANT
DESTITUTE	INCITING	PINNACLE	SPECTACLES	WIELD
DICTATES	INORDINATE	RAIDING	STAMPEDE	WRINGING

Witness Vocabulary Crossword 1

Across

2. Institution for the treatment of certain chronic diseases or various nervous or mental disorders
5. Carry on despite hardships
7. Reprimand or criticize harshly and usually angrily
8. Furiously intense; wild; violent in force
11. Flustered; unnerved; confused
12. Supremely good or beautiful; magnificent
15. Conflict; struggle; clash
17. Typical of country life of country people
19. Irritated; annoyed
20. Exercise power, or influence as in ruling or dominating
21. Conducting a surprise attack on another's property with the purpose of taking goods
22. Insane person

Down

1. Without principles
2. Firm; strong; having endurance
3. Tame; gentle; kind
4. A cross with the form of Jesus on it
6. Misleading; to make others believe something that is not true
9. Rule or hold authority; dominate with power or influence
10. Looked intently, searchingly, or with difficulty
12. Lacking food, clothing, and shelter
13. Stirring up, encouraging or prompting into action
14. Around or twisted together
16. Symbol burned on with a hot iron
18. Recommending; suggesting
19. On the alert; watchful

Witness Vocabulary Crossword 1 Answer Key

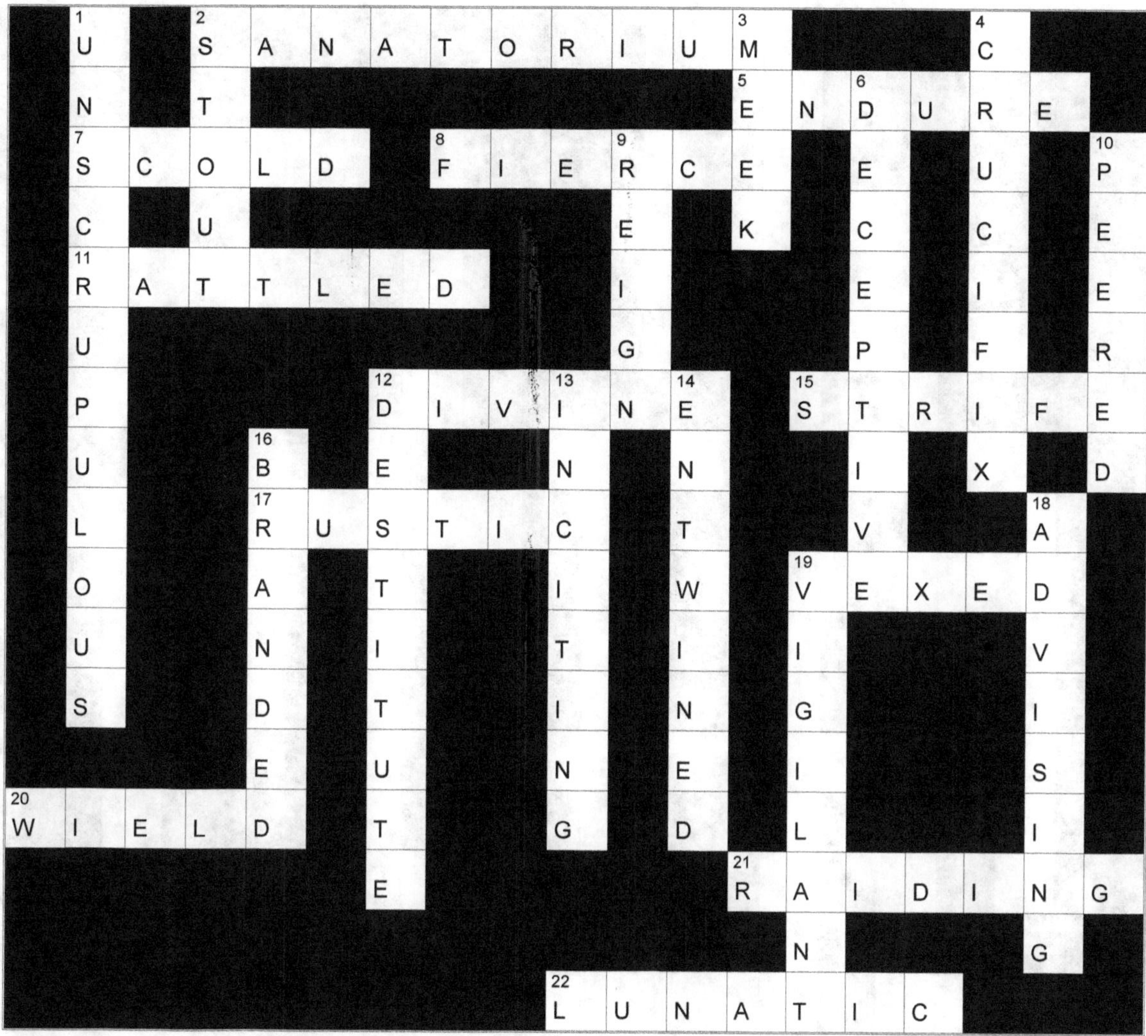

Across
2. Institution for the treatment of certain chronic diseases or various nervous or mental disorders
5. Carry on despite hardships
7. Reprimand or criticize harshly and usually angrily
8. Furiously intense; wild; violent in force
11. Flustered; unnerved; confused
12. Supremely good or beautiful; magnificent
15. Conflict; struggle; clash
17. Typical of country life of country people
19. Irritated; annoyed
20. Exercise power, or influence as in ruling or dominating
21. Conducting a surprise attack on another's property with the purpose of taking goods
22. Insane person

Down
1. Without principles
2. Firm; strong; having endurance
3. Tame; gentle; kind
4. A cross with the form of Jesus on it
6. Misleading; to make others believe something that is not true
9. Rule or hold authority; dominate with power or influence
10. Looked intently, searchingly, or with difficulty
12. Lacking food, clothing, and shelter
13. Stirring up, encouraging or prompting into action
14. Around or twisted together
16. Symbol burned on with a hot iron
18. Recommending; suggesting
19. On the alert; watchful

Witness Vocabulary Crossword 2

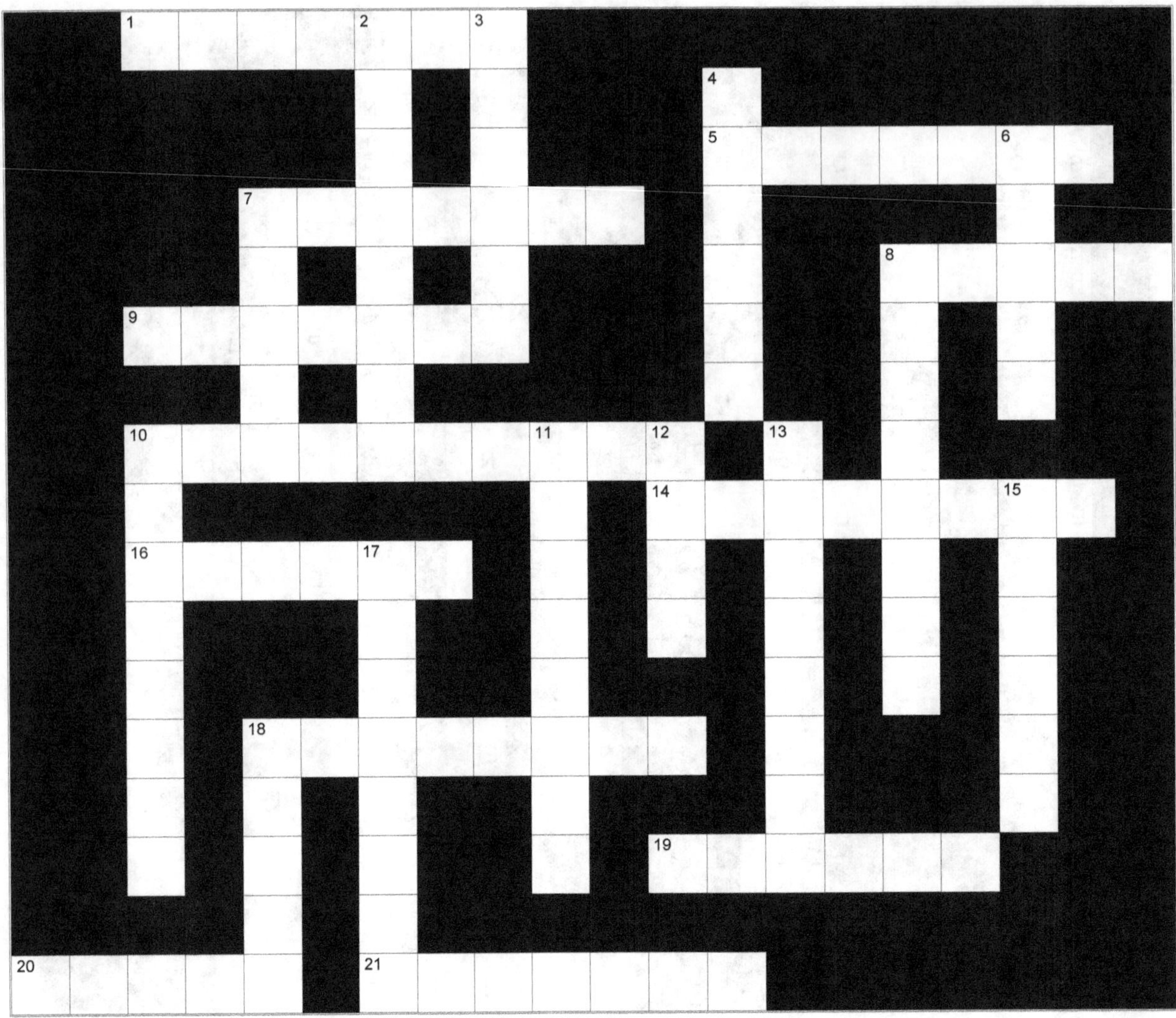

Across

1. Feels sorrow or distress
5. Nonsense; worthless material; garbage
7. Conducting a surprise attack on another's property with the purpose of taking goods
8. Reprimand or criticize harshly and usually angrily
9. Large body of troops; a military unit
10. Institution for the treatment of certain chronic diseases or various nervous or mental disorders
14. Around or twisted together
16. Typical of country life of country people
18. Extracting or expelling by twisting or compression
19. Looked intently, searchingly, or with difficulty
20. Irritated; annoyed
21. Muttering a complaint

Down

2. On the alert; watchful
3. Conflict; struggle; clash
4. Encouraging
6. Firm; strong; having endurance
7. Rule or hold authority; dominate with power or influence
8. Showing good sense or sound judgment
10. Walked in a pompous way
11. Very impressive because of great size, stately appearance, or dignity
12. Tame; gentle; kind
13. Frenzied rush of a mass of people
15. Carry on despite hardships
17. Stirring up, encouraging or prompting into action
18. Exercise power, or influence as in ruling or dominating

Witness Vocabulary Crossword 2 Answer Key

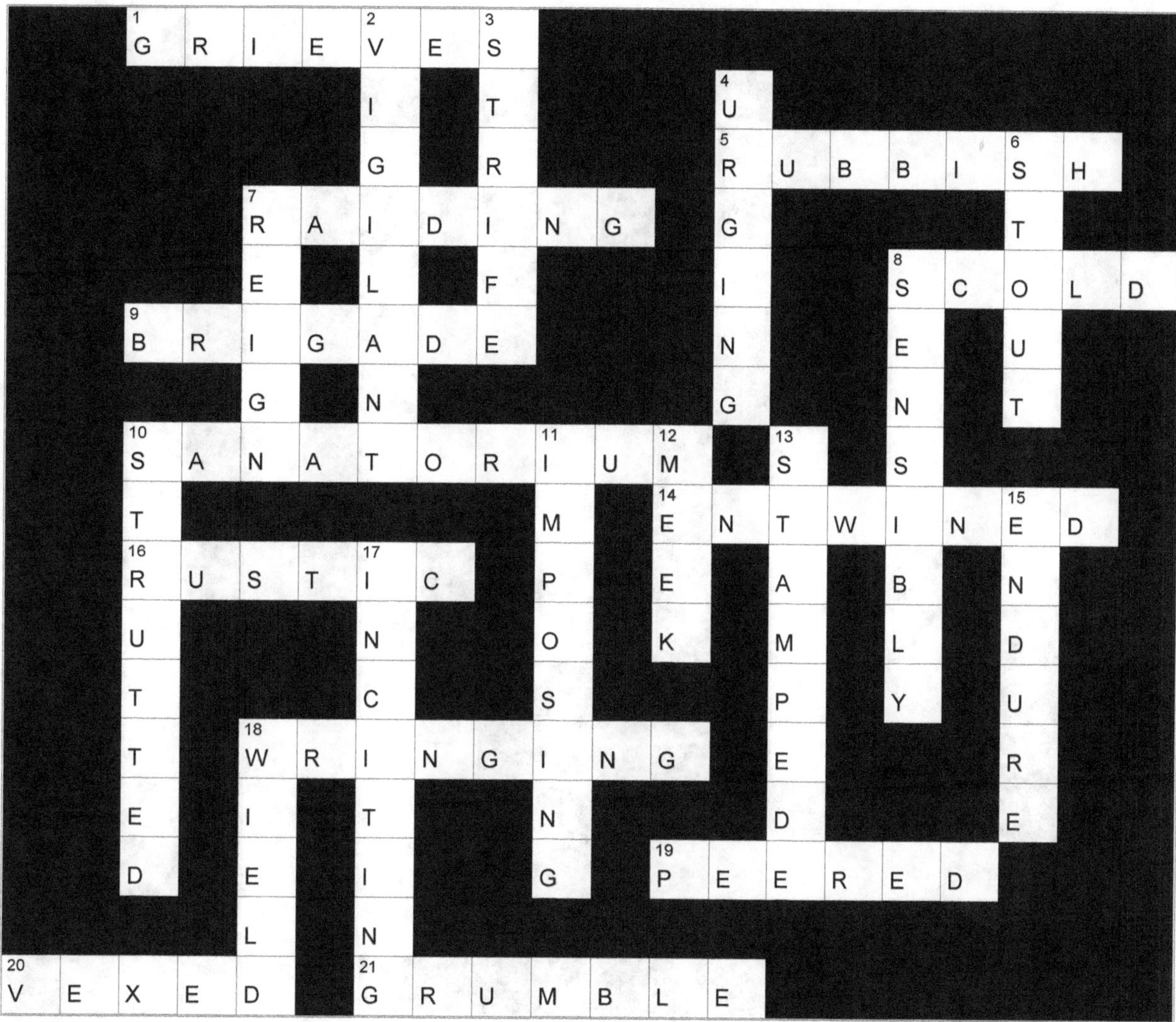

Across
1. Feels sorrow or distress
5. Nonsense; worthless material; garbage
7. Conducting a surprise attack on another's property with the purpose of taking goods
8. Reprimand or criticize harshly and usually angrily
9. Large body of troops; a military unit
10. Institution for the treatment of certain chronic diseases or various nervous or mental disorders
14. Around or twisted together
16. Typical of country life of country people
18. Extracting or expelling by twisting or compression
19. Looked intently, searchingly, or with difficulty
20. Irritated; annoyed
21. Muttering a complaint

Down
2. On the alert; watchful
3. Conflict; struggle; clash
4. Encouraging
6. Firm; strong; having endurance
7. Rule or hold authority; dominate with power or influence
8. Showing good sense or sound judgment
10. Walked in a pompous way
11. Very impressive because of great size, stately appearance, or dignity
12. Tame; gentle; kind
13. Frenzied rush of a mass of people
15. Carry on despite hardships
17. Stirring up, encouraging or prompting into action
18. Exercise power, or influence as in ruling or dominating

Witness Vocabulary Crossword 3

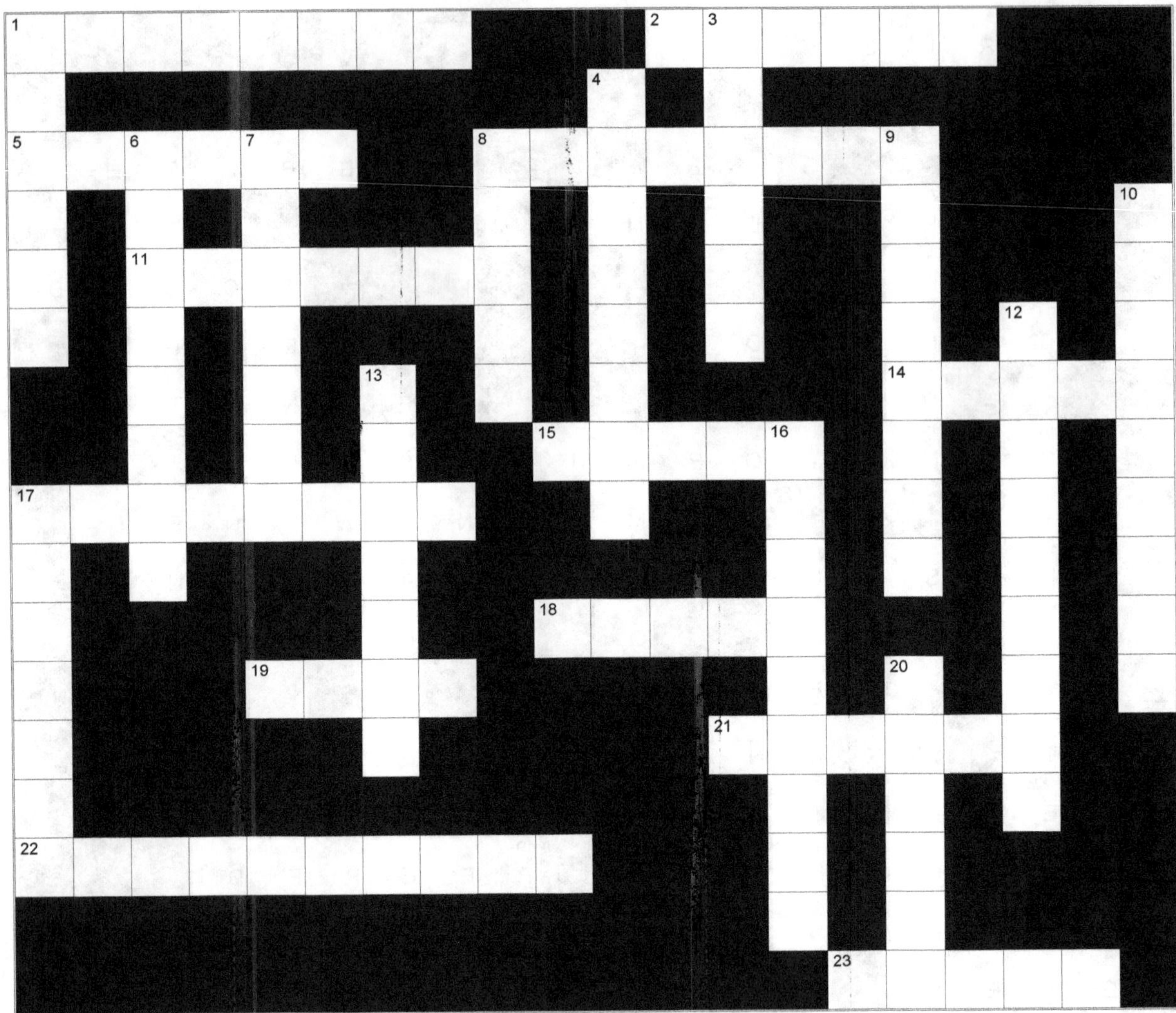

Across

1. Around or twisted together
2. Typical of country life of country people
5. Supremely good or beautiful; magnificent
8. Extracting or expelling by twisting or compression
11. Muttering a complaint
14. Reprimand or criticize harshly and usually angrily
15. Irritated; annoyed
17. Awkwardly tall or long-limbed
18. Firm; strong; having endurance
19. Tame; gentle; kind
21. Conflict; struggle; clash
22. Eyeglasses
23. Rule or hold authority; dominate with power or influence

Down

1. Carry on despite hardships
3. Encouraging
4. Guiding principles
6. On the alert; watchful
7. Belonging to neither side in a controversy
8. Exercise power, or influence as in ruling or dominating
9. Waterproof boot or shoe
10. Future state of the wicked; damnation; hell
12. The way a person acts, especially from the standpoint of morality and ethics
13. Hanged, as by a mob, without due process of the law
16. Lacking food, clothing, and shelter
17. Feels sorrow or distress
20. Furiously intense; wild; violent in force

Witness Vocabulary Crossword 3 Answer Key

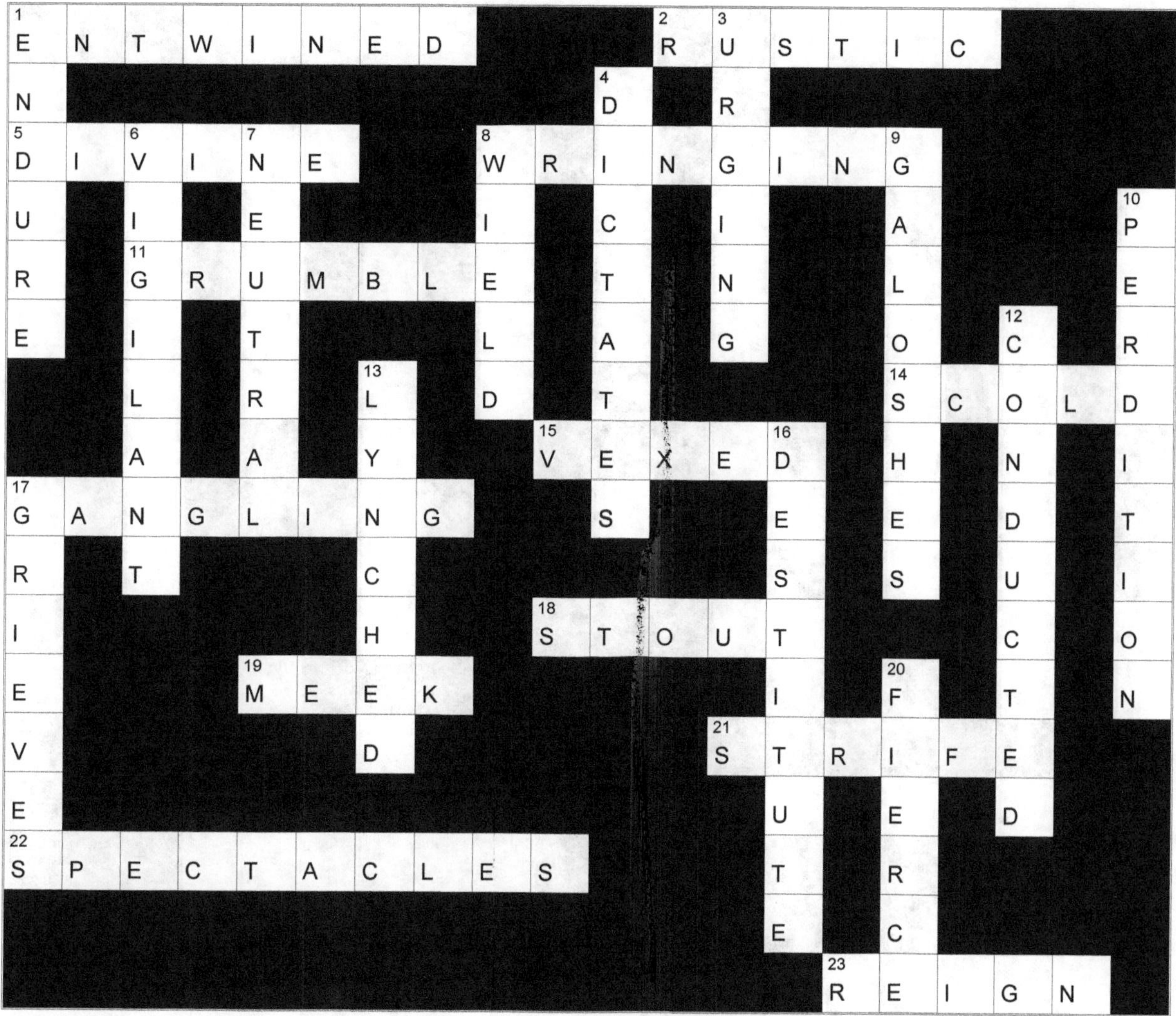

Across

1. Around or twisted together
2. Typical of country life of country people
5. Supremely good or beautiful; magnificent
8. Extracting or expelling by twisting or compression
11. Muttering a complaint
14. Reprimand or criticize harshly and usually angrily
15. Irritated; annoyed
17. Awkwardly tall or long-limbed
18. Firm; strong; having endurance
19. Tame; gentle; kind
21. Conflict; struggle; clash
22. Eyeglasses
23. Rule or hold authority; dominate with power or influence

Down

1. Carry on despite hardships
3. Encouraging
4. Guiding principles
6. On the alert; watchful
7. Belonging to neither side in a controversy
8. Exercise power, or influence as in ruling or dominating
9. Waterproof boot or shoe
10. Future state of the wicked; damnation; hell
12. The way a person acts, especially from the standpoint of morality and ethics
13. Hanged, as by a mob, without due process of the law
16. Lacking food, clothing, and shelter
17. Feels sorrow or distress
20. Furiously intense; wild; violent in force

Witness Vocabulary Crossword 4

Across

1. Large body of troops; a military unit
2. Showing good sense or sound judgment
5. Recommending; suggesting
8. Carry on despite hardships
10. Conducting a surprise attack on another's property with the purpose of taking goods
12. Supremely good or beautiful; magnificent
15. Tame; gentle; kind
17. Awkwardly tall or long-limbed
18. Reprimand or criticize harshly and usually angrily
19. Firm; strong; having endurance
20. Around or twisted together
21. Furiously intense; wild; violent in force
22. Eyeglasses

Down

1. Symbol burned on with a hot iron
2. Conflict; struggle; clash
3. Hanged, as by a mob, without due process of the law
4. Future state of the wicked; damnation; hell
6. Muttering a complaint
7. Guiding principles
9. Without principles
11. Waterproof boot or shoe
13. On the alert; watchful
14. Belonging to neither side in a controversy
16. Typical of country life of country people
17. Feels sorrow or distress

Witness Vocabulary Crossword 4 Answer Key

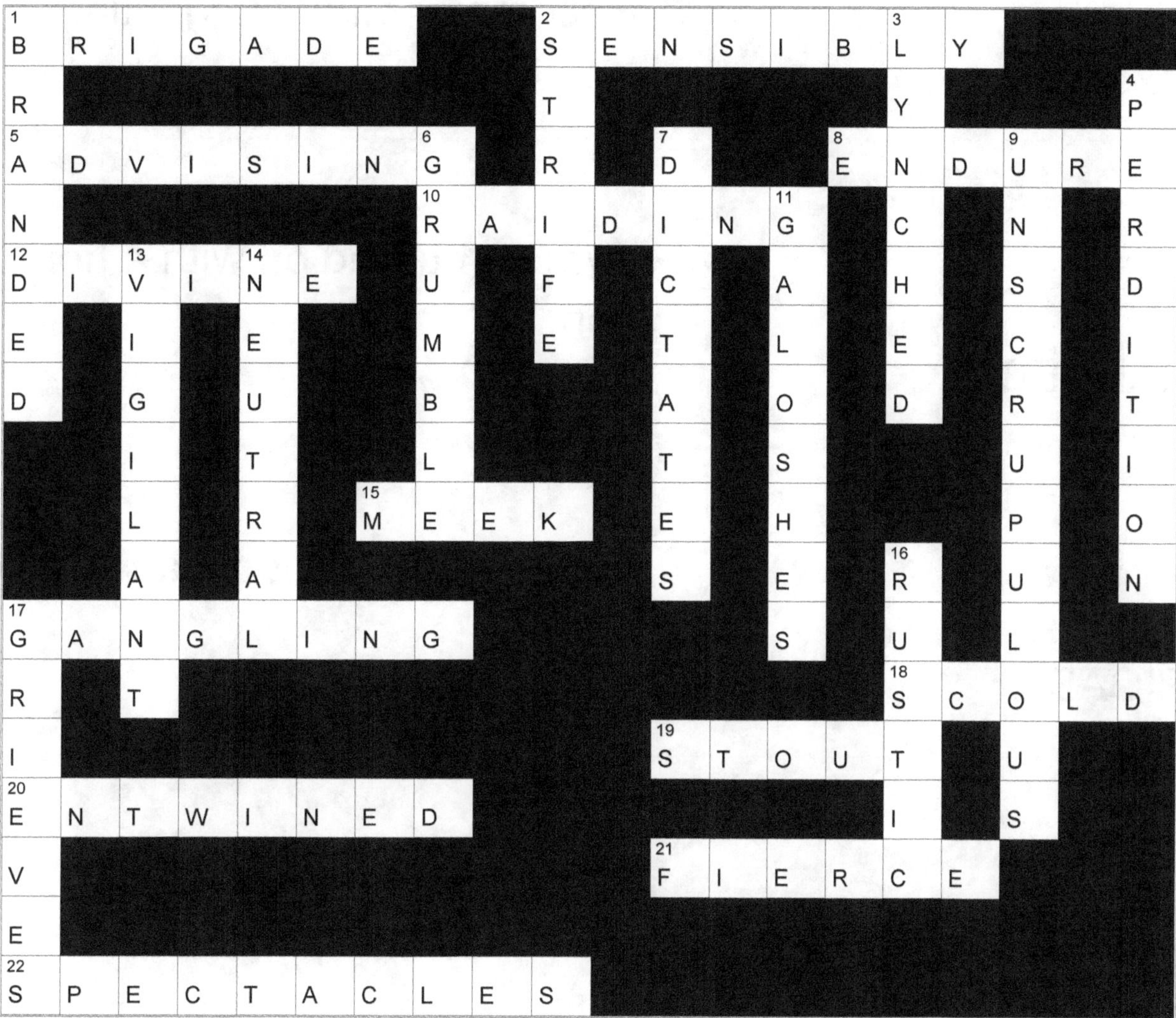

Across

1. Large body of troops; a military unit
2. Showing good sense or sound judgment
5. Recommending; suggesting
8. Carry on despite hardships
10. Conducting a surprise attack on another's property with the purpose of taking goods
12. Supremely good or beautiful; magnificent
15. Tame; gentle; kind
17. Awkwardly tall or long-limbed
18. Reprimand or criticize harshly and usually angrily
19. Firm; strong; having endurance
20. Around or twisted together
21. Furiously intense; wild; violent in force
22. Eyeglasses

Down

1. Symbol burned on with a hot iron
2. Conflict; struggle; clash
3. Hanged, as by a mob, without due process of the law
4. Future state of the wicked; damnation; hell
6. Muttering a complaint
7. Guiding principles
9. Without principles
11. Waterproof boot or shoe
13. On the alert; watchful
14. Belonging to neither side in a controversy
16. Typical of country life of country people
17. Feels sorrow or distress

ADVISING	Recommending; suggesting
BRANDED	Symbol burned on with a hot iron
BRIGADE	Large body of troops; a military unit
CLERGYMAN	Christian minister
CONDUCTED	The way a person acts, especially from the standpoint of morality and ethics
CONSTABLE	Peace officer with less authority than a sheriff

CRUCIFIX	A cross with the form of Jesus on it
DECEPTIVE	Misleading; to make others believe something that is not true
DESTITUTE	Lacking food, clothing, and shelter
DICTATES	Guiding principles
DIVINE	Supremely good or beautiful; magnificent
ENDURE	Carry on despite hardships

ENTWINED	Around or twisted together
FIERCE	Furiously intense; wild; violent in force
GALOSHES	Waterproof boot or shoe
GANGLING	Awkwardly tall or long-limbed
GRIEVES	Feels sorrow or distress
GRUMBLE	Muttering a complaint

IMPOSING	Very impressive because of great size, stately appearance, or dignity
INCITING	Stirring up, encouraging or prompting into action
INORDINATE	Exceeding reasonable limits; uncontrolled
LUNATIC	Insane person
LYNCHED	Hanged, as by a mob, without due process of the law
MEEK	Tame; gentle; kind

NEUTRAL	Belonging to neither side in a controversy
PEERED	Looked intently, searchingly, or with difficulty
PERDITION	Future state of the wicked; damnation; hell
PERSECUTION	Punishment or harassment usually severe in nature based on race, religion, or political views
PETITION	Formal request
PINNACLE	The highest point, as with success, power, or fame

RAIDING	Conducting a surprise attack on another's property with the purpose of taking goods
RATTLED	Flustered; unnerved; confused
REIGN	Rule or hold authority; dominate with power or influence
RUBBISH	Nonsense; worthless material; garbage
RUSTIC	Typical of country life of country people
SANATORIUM	Institution for the treatment of certain chronic diseases or various nervous or mental disorders

SCOLD	Reprimand or criticize harshly and usually angrily
SENSIBLY	Showing good sense or sound judgment
SPECTACLES	Eyeglasses
STAMPEDE	Frenzied rush of a mass of people
STOUT	Firm; strong; having endurance
STRIFE	Conflict; struggle; clash

STRUTTED	Walked in a pompous way
UNSCRUPULOUS	Without principles
URGING	Encouraging
VEXED	Irritated; annoyed
VIGILANT	On the alert; watchful
WIELD	Exercise power, or influence as in ruling or dominating

WRINGING	Extracting or expelling by twisting or compression

WITNESS VOCAB

GANGLING	PINNACLE	RATTLED	REIGN	PEERED
VEXED	CONDUCTED	MEEK	ENDURE	PERDITION
GALOSHES	WRINGING	FREE SPACE	PETITION	BRANDED
DESTITUTE	INORDINATE	STOUT	VIGILANT	INCITING
RAIDING	RUBBISH	PERSECUTION	GRUMBLE	BRIGADE

WITNESS VOCAB

STAMPEDE	ENTWINED	RUSTIC	STRIFE	STRUTTED
SANATORIUM	GRIEVES	SPECTACLES	IMPOSING	SENSIBLY
DIVINE	LUNATIC	FREE SPACE	CLERGYMAN	DICTATES
SCOLD	ADVISING	CRUCIFIX	URGING	FIERCE
WIELD	NEUTRAL	CONSTABLE	DECEPTIVE	BRIGADE

WITNESS VOCAB

RUBBISH	MEEK	CLERGYMAN	FIERCE	VEXED
LUNATIC	GANGLING	ENTWINED	URGING	RAIDING
SENSIBLY	WRINGING	FREE SPACE	DECEPTIVE	GALOSHES
DIVINE	PINNACLE	STAMPEDE	BRIGADE	ADVISING
RUSTIC	GRIEVES	PERSECUTION	BRANDED	PEERED

WITNESS VOCAB

STRIFE	DESTITUTE	CONSTABLE	VIGILANT	STRUTTED
SCOLD	UNSCRUPULOUS	ENDURE	GRUMBLE	PERDITION
DICTATES	INORDINATE	FREE SPACE	INCITING	CRUCIFIX
RATTLED	IMPOSING	SPECTACLES	LYNCHED	PETITION
STOUT	NEUTRAL	SANATORIUM	CONDUCTED	PEERED

WITNESS VOCAB

NEUTRAL	SPECTACLES	LYNCHED	PINNACLE	GANGLING
WIELD	SENSIBLY	INCITING	SANATORIUM	CONDUCTED
RAIDING	CLERGYMAN	FREE SPACE	CONSTABLE	STOUT
REIGN	ENTWINED	DECEPTIVE	MEEK	GRIEVES
STRUTTED	RUBBISH	DICTATES	RATTLED	UNSCRUPULOUS

WITNESS VOCAB

URGING	DESTITUTE	RUSTIC	GALOSHES	PERDITION
ADVISING	PETITION	DIVINE	VEXED	STAMPEDE
PERSECUTION	LUNATIC	FREE SPACE	BRANDED	GRUMBLE
PEERED	BRIGADE	VIGILANT	SCOLD	INORDINATE
STRIFE	IMPOSING	ENDURE	FIERCE	UNSCRUPULOUS

WITNESS VOCAB

UNSCRUPULOUS	STRIFE	GRIEVES	ADVISING	PEERED
DICTATES	RUSTIC	WIELD	SENSIBLY	CONSTABLE
STRUTTED	PINNACLE	FREE SPACE	RUBBISH	STAMPEDE
BRANDED	RAIDING	BRIGADE	DIVINE	CLERGYMAN
DECEPTIVE	URGING	ENTWINED	NEUTRAL	INCITING

WITNESS VOCAB

PETITION	SPECTACLES	PERSECUTION	CONDUCTED	LUNATIC
STOUT	GALOSHES	GRUMBLE	CRUCIFIX	WRINGING
REIGN	GANGLING	FREE SPACE	DESTITUTE	MEEK
RATTLED	SANATORIUM	PERDITION	IMPOSING	SCOLD
VEXED	VIGILANT	FIERCE	ENDURE	INCITING

WITNESS VOCAB

INCITING	SENSIBLY	SPECTACLES	WIELD	VIGILANT
IMPOSING	PETITION	PERDITION	CONSTABLE	ENDURE
ADVISING	GANGLING	FREE SPACE	UNSCRUPULOUS	STRUTTED
BRANDED	PERSECUTION	GRUMBLE	RUSTIC	RUBBISH
CLERGYMAN	STAMPEDE	STOUT	RATTLED	BRIGADE

WITNESS VOCAB

FIERCE	ENTWINED	SCOLD	INORDINATE	DICTATES
DESTITUTE	DECEPTIVE	NEUTRAL	CRUCIFIX	PINNACLE
GRIEVES	VEXED	FREE SPACE	PEERED	LYNCHED
SANATORIUM	REIGN	URGING	DIVINE	MEEK
RAIDING	GALOSHES	WRINGING	CONDUCTED	BRIGADE

WITNESS VOCAB

NEUTRAL	CRUCIFIX	INORDINATE	BRIGADE	UNSCRUPULOUS
CONSTABLE	STOUT	LYNCHED	GALOSHES	SENSIBLY
URGING	DESTITUTE	FREE SPACE	ENDURE	RAIDING
LUNATIC	VEXED	RUBBISH	STAMPEDE	BRANDED
STRUTTED	SANATORIUM	PERSECUTION	WIELD	RUSTIC

WITNESS VOCAB

VIGILANT	DIVINE	GRUMBLE	REIGN	GRIEVES
ADVISING	SCOLD	IMPOSING	DICTATES	PEERED
PINNACLE	PETITION	FREE SPACE	FIERCE	GANGLING
CONDUCTED	ENTWINED	PERDITION	RATTLED	DECEPTIVE
WRINGING	MEEK	CLERGYMAN	STRIFE	RUSTIC

WITNESS VOCAB

INORDINATE	DESTITUTE	CLERGYMAN	ENDURE	VIGILANT
STOUT	URGING	PINNACLE	CRUCIFIX	SANATORIUM
PEERED	IMPOSING	FREE SPACE	CONDUCTED	ENTWINED
GRIEVES	LYNCHED	WRINGING	UNSCRUPULOUS	RUBBISH
SENSIBLY	WIELD	RUSTIC	RAIDING	REIGN

WITNESS VOCAB

GRUMBLE	DECEPTIVE	SCOLD	PERSECUTION	STRUTTED
DIVINE	DICTATES	SPECTACLES	INCITING	NEUTRAL
GALOSHES	BRIGADE	FREE SPACE	PERDITION	LUNATIC
STRIFE	VEXED	ADVISING	FIERCE	BRANDED
GANGLING	MEEK	PETITION	CONSTABLE	REIGN

WITNESS VOCAB

PEERED	STOUT	RATTLED	REIGN	GANGLING
SCOLD	URGING	BRANDED	ENDURE	ENTWINED
FIERCE	SPECTACLES	FREE SPACE	UNSCRUPULOUS	LUNATIC
BRIGADE	STRIFE	DECEPTIVE	NEUTRAL	DICTATES
STAMPEDE	CONSTABLE	RAIDING	PERSECUTION	VIGILANT

WITNESS VOCAB

STRUTTED	VEXED	WIELD	WRINGING	GALOSHES
SANATORIUM	PINNACLE	RUBBISH	LYNCHED	CONDUCTED
DIVINE	GRUMBLE	FREE SPACE	MEEK	PETITION
PERDITION	DESTITUTE	INCITING	SENSIBLY	GRIEVES
CLERGYMAN	CRUCIFIX	ADVISING	INORDINATE	VIGILANT

WITNESS VOCAB

DECEPTIVE	CRUCIFIX	STOUT	PINNACLE	STRIFE
PEERED	IMPOSING	STAMPEDE	GRIEVES	VEXED
SCOLD	FIERCE	FREE SPACE	LYNCHED	GANGLING
INCITING	DESTITUTE	CONDUCTED	PERSECUTION	GALOSHES
SANATORIUM	STRUTTED	DIVINE	WRINGING	RATTLED

WITNESS VOCAB

UNSCRUPULOUS	RAIDING	DICTATES	BRIGADE	RUBBISH
PETITION	WIELD	URGING	BRANDED	RUSTIC
LUNATIC	SPECTACLES	FREE SPACE	REIGN	CLERGYMAN
ADVISING	PERDITION	INORDINATE	VIGILANT	GRUMBLE
SENSIBLY	NEUTRAL	ENTWINED	ENDURE	RATTLED

WITNESS VOCAB

WIELD	GANGLING	STRIFE	RAIDING	INORDINATE
STRUTTED	DESTITUTE	SPECTACLES	RUSTIC	IMPOSING
PEERED	PERDITION	FREE SPACE	FIERCE	LYNCHED
RUBBISH	RATTLED	ADVISING	BRANDED	INCITING
ENTWINED	REIGN	DIVINE	GRIEVES	CONDUCTED

WITNESS VOCAB

BRIGADE	SANATORIUM	MEEK	DICTATES	CLERGYMAN
GALOSHES	GRUMBLE	VIGILANT	ENDURE	PERSECUTION
CRUCIFIX	PINNACLE	FREE SPACE	CONSTABLE	WRINGING
LUNATIC	STOUT	UNSCRUPULOUS	SCOLD	VEXED
PETITION	SENSIBLY	URGING	STAMPEDE	CONDUCTED

WITNESS VOCAB

RUBBISH	INORDINATE	IMPOSING	REIGN	UNSCRUPULOUS
ENDURE	PERSECUTION	MEEK	DICTATES	NEUTRAL
SPECTACLES	SCOLD	FREE SPACE	URGING	PETITION
RUSTIC	WRINGING	CONSTABLE	SENSIBLY	ADVISING
RAIDING	LUNATIC	FIERCE	CRUCIFIX	PEERED

WITNESS VOCAB

GRIEVES	STRIFE	STAMPEDE	GALOSHES	DESTITUTE
PINNACLE	DECEPTIVE	CLERGYMAN	VEXED	GANGLING
VIGILANT	CONDUCTED	FREE SPACE	DIVINE	INCITING
WIELD	GRUMBLE	STRUTTED	SANATORIUM	STOUT
ENTWINED	LYNCHED	BRANDED	PERDITION	PEERED

WITNESS VOCAB

WRINGING	URGING	LYNCHED	PERDITION	VIGILANT
MEEK	GANGLING	GRIEVES	SCOLD	IMPOSING
SPECTACLES	UNSCRUPULOUS	FREE SPACE	PERSECUTION	STRUTTED
PEERED	BRIGADE	RAIDING	ADVISING	VEXED
NEUTRAL	WIELD	ENDURE	DIVINE	BRANDED

WITNESS VOCAB

FIERCE	RUBBISH	GALOSHES	PINNACLE	PETITION
GRUMBLE	STAMPEDE	CRUCIFIX	STRIFE	CONDUCTED
DICTATES	REIGN	FREE SPACE	RATTLED	STOUT
RUSTIC	SANATORIUM	ENTWINED	INORDINATE	DECEPTIVE
SENSIBLY	DESTITUTE	INCITING	LUNATIC	BRANDED

WITNESS VOCAB

UNSCRUPULOUS	PETITION	BRANDED	INORDINATE	CONSTABLE
CRUCIFIX	ADVISING	PINNACLE	STRIFE	SPECTACLES
STOUT	REIGN	FREE SPACE	SANATORIUM	DICTATES
VEXED	SCOLD	LUNATIC	CONDUCTED	SENSIBLY
BRIGADE	VIGILANT	PEERED	RUSTIC	GALOSHES

WITNESS VOCAB

FIERCE	GANGLING	CLERGYMAN	GRUMBLE	INCITING
RATTLED	URGING	DESTITUTE	NEUTRAL	ENDURE
WRINGING	RUBBISH	FREE SPACE	PERSECUTION	STRUTTED
PERDITION	STAMPEDE	LYNCHED	DIVINE	GRIEVES
DECEPTIVE	ENTWINED	IMPOSING	MEEK	GALOSHES

WITNESS VOCAB

WRINGING	UNSCRUPULOUS	ENDURE	WIELD	PEERED
CONDUCTED	MEEK	IMPOSING	STRUTTED	INCITING
ADVISING	RUSTIC	FREE SPACE	CONSTABLE	NEUTRAL
INORDINATE	FIERCE	SCOLD	PERDITION	GANGLING
SANATORIUM	STAMPEDE	CRUCIFIX	BRANDED	REIGN

WITNESS VOCAB

DESTITUTE	VEXED	DICTATES	BRIGADE	SENSIBLY
LYNCHED	CLERGYMAN	STRIFE	STOUT	ENTWINED
SPECTACLES	GRUMBLE	FREE SPACE	GALOSHES	URGING
RATTLED	VIGILANT	PETITION	RUBBISH	PINNACLE
GRIEVES	DECEPTIVE	RAIDING	LUNATIC	REIGN

WITNESS VOCAB

PETITION	VEXED	STOUT	WRINGING	LYNCHED
GRIEVES	VIGILANT	SANATORIUM	DECEPTIVE	PEERED
PERDITION	GANGLING	FREE SPACE	PINNACLE	PERSECUTION
INORDINATE	RATTLED	GRUMBLE	CONDUCTED	CONSTABLE
NEUTRAL	DIVINE	STAMPEDE	DESTITUTE	SENSIBLY

WITNESS VOCAB

REIGN	ADVISING	IMPOSING	MEEK	BRANDED
BRIGADE	RAIDING	CLERGYMAN	STRIFE	RUSTIC
FIERCE	RUBBISH	FREE SPACE	INCITING	LUNATIC
URGING	SPECTACLES	ENTWINED	CRUCIFIX	SCOLD
STRUTTED	GALOSHES	DICTATES	UNSCRUPULOUS	SENSIBLY

WITNESS VOCAB

CRUCIFIX	PETITION	CONDUCTED	MEEK	PEERED
STRUTTED	STOUT	GRUMBLE	STAMPEDE	INORDINATE
INCITING	DECEPTIVE	FREE SPACE	PINNACLE	CLERGYMAN
VEXED	ADVISING	RATTLED	NEUTRAL	PERDITION
SPECTACLES	REIGN	RAIDING	CONSTABLE	BRIGADE

WITNESS VOCAB

DICTATES	WRINGING	DIVINE	BRANDED	GANGLING
WIELD	IMPOSING	UNSCRUPULOUS	ENTWINED	SANATORIUM
STRIFE	GRIEVES	FREE SPACE	LYNCHED	VIGILANT
ENDURE	DESTITUTE	SENSIBLY	RUSTIC	SCOLD
GALOSHES	LUNATIC	RUBBISH	FIERCE	BRIGADE

www.ingramcontent.com/pod-product-compliance
Lightning Source LLC
Chambersburg PA
CBHW082102090726
47910CB00008B/2562

9781602494732